António Sarmento Batista

Logistic Regression

An introduction to a statistical model with an example on

Revolving Credit

Copyright © 2014 **António Sarmento Batista**
All rights reserved.

ISBN: 1503353559
ISBN 13: 9781503353558
Library of Congress Control Number:
LCCN Imprint Name:

António Sarmento Batista

Logistic Regression

An introduction to a statistical model with an example on

Revolving Credit

Copyright © 2014 **António Sarmento Batista**
All rights reserved.

ISBN: 1503353559
ISBN 13: 9781503353558
Library of Congress Control Number:
LCCN Imprint Name:

To my faithful friend Tosh Brown.

Contents

Preliminary Notes 11
   Objective 11
   Case Study 11
   Consumer Credit 11
   Statistical Methods 12

Chapter 1 13

Introduction 13

Chapter 2 17

Some Statistical Models Used in the Default Prediction 17
   2.1 Discriminant Analysis 17
   2.2 Univariate Discriminant Analysis 19
   2.3 Multivariate Discriminant Analysis 19
   2.4 Discriminant Function 22

Chapter 3 25

Logistic Regression 25
   3.1 Logistic-Regression Models (Logit) 25
   3.3 Logistic Model 28
   3.4 Transforming Probabilities into Odds 28
   3.5 Natural Logarithm of Odds 29
   3.6 Meaning of Odds 30
   3.7 Logged Odds (or Logit) 32
   3.8 Logit Properties 32

3.9 Obtaining Probabilities through Logits 34

3.10 An Alternative Formula to Calculate Probability 36

Chapter 4 37

General Procedure in Parameters Estimation 37

4.1 Introduction 37

4.2 Maximum-Likelihood Method 37

4.3 Step-by-Step Logistic-Regression Techniques 40
    4.3.1 Forward Selection 40
    4.3.2 Backward Elimination 40
    4.3.3 Combination of Previous Techniques (Stepwise) 40

4.4 Classification of Variable Characteristics 42

4.5 Estimation by Maximum Likelihood vs. Discriminant Analysis 43

4.6 Likelihood Function $LF\theta$ and Its Use in the Procedure of Maximum Likelihood ($LFMax$) 44

4.7 Log-Likelihood Function (LLF) 51

4.8 Parameters Estimation 53

Chapter 5 55

Tests of Significance Using Log-Likelihood Values 55

5.1 Difference between Probability and Likelihood 55

5.2 Likelihood Ratio Test 55

5.3 Tests of Significance 57

Chapter 6 65

Evaluation of the Logistic Model 65

6.1 Introduction 65

6.2 R^2 Statistic 65

6.3 R^2 Pseudo Statistic 71

  6.3.1 McFadden's R^2 73
  6.3.2 Cox and Snell's R^2 74
 6.4 Statistical Software Packages for Logistic Regression 76
 6.5 Z-Wald Test 76

Chapter 7 81

ROC Curves 81

 7.1 Introduction 81
 7.2 Signal-Detection Theory 81
  7.2.1 Signal Detection 83
 7.3 Statistical Theory 86
 7.4 Confusion Matrix 90
 7.5 Computer-Program Outputs 93
 7.6 ROC Curves Graphic Layout 96
 7.7 Area Under ROC Curve (AUROC) 101
 7.8 Type I and Type II Errors 104

Chapter 8 111

Case Study: Logistic-Regression Application to Revolving Credit 111

 8.1 Methodology 111
 8.2 Data Analysis 112
 8.3 Distinction between Good and Bad Payers 115
 8.4 Grouping of Variables According to Their Nature 117
 8.5 Variables Interpretation 117
  8.5.1 Description vs. Account State ID 118
  8.5.2 Description vs. Account Class ID 119
  8.5.3 Overdue Accounts for More than Sixty Days vs. Ninety Days 121
  8.5.4 Gender 122
  8.5.5 Marital Status 124
  8.5.7 Credit Limit 127

8.6 Data Transformation 130

8.7 Variables Characterization by Descriptive Statistics Measures 133

8.8 Application of Logit Model to Sample Data 135
    8.8.1 Model Application to In-Sample Data 135
    8.8.2 Quality Evaluation of the Adjustment 136
    8.8.3 Marginal Effects of the Explanatory Variables on the Probability of a User Being a Good Payer 140
    8.8.4 Heteroscedasticity Errors Test 144

8.9 Model Validation through Out-of-Sample 146

8.10 Conclusions 147

References **148**

Preliminary Notes

Objective

The purpose of this book is to present an introduction to the statistical *logistic-regression* model and apply its use to a case study.

Case Study

The case study presented in chapter 8 is an application of the *logistic-regression* model to *consumer credit*, and it aims to build a strong statistical predictive model able to predict failure of payment by users of credit cards.

Consumer Credit

This type of credit (to consumers), which is specifically granted to credit-card users, is called *revolving credit*, and its repayment to the financial institution does not have a fixed number of payments. The *borrower* (e.g., the credit-card user) may use or withdraw funds from the credit institution, up to a certain credit limit amount that has been previously granted. The repayment to the *lender* (the credit institution) is via (total or partial) periodic payments, plus interest.

The frequency of these payments is usually monthly, and their value is subject to a minimum amount, depending on the value of the total outstanding debt. The credit limit granted to credit-card users is calculated by a set of criteria judgments, including user *characteristics* combined with the payments history and his/her behavior in terms of punctuality and regularity.

The calculations for achieving the credit limit and credit-granting decisions are supported by risk manager and use statistical methods, which may facilitate and help him/her to make assertive decisions.

At the end of 2012, there were 1.1 credit cards per person in Portugal, which means about 11,000,000 credit cards. The issue of consumer credit default, in Portugal, has been experiencing strong growth since 2005, but it has recorded a slight decline in 2013, according to Banco de Portugal (B4.1.4 loans of other monetary financial institutions to private individuals), as illustrated below.

Table 1. Evolution of consumer credit to bad debt in Portugal since 2004

	CONSUMER CREDIT IN PORTUGAL (€)		
	Loan	Bad debts	Percentage of bad debts (%)
Dec 2004	9 059 000 000	454 000 000	5.01
Dec 2005	9 406 000 000	292 000 000	3.10
Dec 2006	11 379 000 000	369 000 000	3.24
Dec 2007	13 790 000 000	505 000 000	3,66
Dec 2008	15 452 000 000	759 000 000	4,91
Dec 2009	15 731 000 000	1 032 000 000	6,56
Dec 2010	15 484 000 000	1 237 000 000	7,99
Dec 2011	14 987 000 000	1 477 000 000	9,86
Dec 2012	13 371 000 000	1 580 000 000	11,82
Dec 2013	12 075 000 000	1 407 000 000	11,65

Statistical Methods

The improvement of consumer-credit management will undergo more rigorous decision making and application of statistics methods to risk-management default methods. One of the statistical methods used in the prediction of default is the *logistic-regression* model, whose introduction is presented in the following chapter.

Chapter 1

Introduction

Every day, financial institutions present many different situations interesting for statistical purposes. These situations can be measured according to certain variables, whether quantitative or qualitative by nature.

For example, a bank employee working as cashier served forty-five clients on a given day (discrete quantitative variable), with the average service time being ten minutes and forty seconds (continuous variable). Among the forty-five clients served, twenty-five were male and twenty were female (qualitative variable).

Forty-five customers, ten minutes and forty seconds, twenty-five men, and twenty women are data that resulted from the observation of certain elements of a bank cashier workday.

One could briefly say that those figures consist of numbers representing counts or measures and qualitative data, also referred to as categorical data or attribute data and distinguished by any nonnumerical characteristic (such as gender).

Many other events of different nature could happen in a financial institution, including the whole process leading to granting consumer credit. The granting of credit is associated with default risk, or credit risk on the supply side.

Credit risk is inherent to each customer individually. When requesting to borrow money, the customer will receive the decision of the risk manager: "Grant credit," or, "Do not grant credit." It is a decision that takes on a dichotomous outcome, and so the dependent variable (the decision) is dual, or binary. The decision of the risk manager can be given in different ways: "Grant credit/Do not grant credit," "Yes/No," or simply, "1/0," which presents advantages for the model that will be developed over the course of this work.

The risk manager uses a set of information that characterizes the customer profile, including age, gender, income, marital status, occupation, etc., which allowed him/her to justify his/her decision.

We shall designate "age," "gender," "income," "marital status," and so many other *characteristics* as *independent variables* or *explanatory variables*. These are the variables that explain or make up the decision (*explained variable* or *dependent variable*) of the risk manager.

A binary qualitative dependent variable with the values 0 and 1 will be the prediction for a "bad" and "good" payer in an automatic decision system.

Thus, we consider one dichotomous outcome for the credit risk through a binary code (COD) in which "0" represents a high credit risk and "1" a low credit risk. We also will apply with equal significance, the designation of "good," or "fulfiller," as 1, and "bad," or "nonfulfiller," as 0.

Suppose we are interested in evaluating the influence of a particular dichotomous independent variable (i.e., gender) in the dichotomous-dependent variable (COD). The question for this example is to assess the extent that reflects the degree of association of gender (G) with credit risk (COD).

Independent variable:

$G(0)$ – *Female*

$G(1)$ – *Male*

Once gender is a qualitative variable, replace it by a numerical dummy variable (0 and 1), as discussed in section 8.6.

COD (0) – With high risk, defaulting, bad

COD (1) – Reduced risk, compliant, good

Figure 1. Influence of gender characteristic on credit decision.

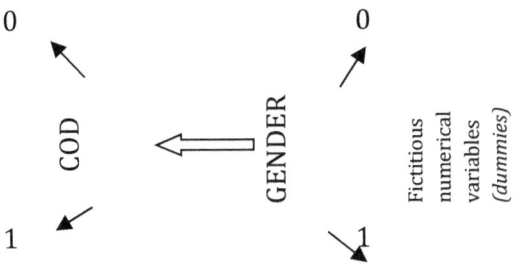

dependent variable   independent variable

or explained variable   or explanatory variable

To assess the magnitude (or extension) in which gender (G) is associated to credit risk (COD), you should take into account other additional variables, such as age, income, marital status, etc, which are not, in this case, the primary interest. Designate those three control variables as C_1, C_2, C_3.

In this example, the variable G (gender), together with the control variables, represents a set of independent variables intended to be used to describe or predict the dichotomous-dependent variable COD.

To illustrate the extent (or the magnitude of the influence) of gender (G) associated to credit risk (COD), we represent:

$$\underbrace{COD}_{\text{Dependent variable}} \Longleftarrow \underbrace{G, C_1, C_2, C_3}_{\text{Independent variables}}.$$

More generally, the independent variables can be replaced by $X_1, X_2, X_3, ..., X_k$, where k is the number of variables considered. X values may also be in combinations, such as $C_4 = C_3 \times G$.

Whenever we wish to relate a set of X_s with the dependent variable, we consider a multivariate problem. In the analysis of this type of problem, a given type of mathematical model is usually used for dealing with complex interrelationships among the variables involved.

Logistic regression responds to this problem constituting a mathematical model that can be used to describe the relationship of various X_s with dummy-dependent variable COD (1/0).

However, before examining the *logistic model* in greater detail, it seems appropriate to briefly review the other models also used in the default prediction for better understanding to the preference given to the *logistic model*.

Chapter 2

Some Statistical Models Used in the Default Prediction

The literature on the prediction of default/bankruptcy is no longer recent. Fifty years have passed since the study by Beaver (1966), which is considered as having pioneered the development of this type of predictive research.

Currently there is a series of research papers dealing with this theme, including Jones (1987); Dimitras, Zanakis, and Zopounidis (1996); Altman and Saunders (1998); Balcaen and Ooghe (2004); Altman and Hotchkiss (2006), among others.

Some parametric studies of *credit scoring* often cited in specialized literature rely on the contributions of Beaver (1966), Altman (1968), Ohlson (1980), and Shumway (2001).

As mentioned above, Beaver (1966) is considered the pioneer in predictive models of default, which have allowed him to forecast insolvency of companies. The theory that supports his model can be better understood in the context of cash flow, as Beaver describe it:

> A company is viewed as a reservoir of liquid assets, which is supplied by inflows and drained by outflows. The reservoir serves as a cushion against variations in the cash flows. Here, the financial distress of a company is modeled as a probability that the reservoir will be exhausted, at which point the company will be unable to pay obligations as they fall due.

2.1 Discriminant Analysis

The literature review (Fair Isaac, 2006) emphasizes that the aim in *discriminant analysis* usually has two options: to segment or separate individuals into two or more predefined groups and to classify any new individual in one of those groups. A rule or *discrimination function* is developed based on measures (or variables) associated with each sample of individuals from two or more populations.

As in the *linear regression*, the general approach is to construct a linear combination of predictor variables that will best distinguish (discriminate) the two groups.

The model is presented in the form of multiple formulas, with each one corresponding to a group.[1] The new individual can then be classified or assigned to the correct population, based on the combinations of highest value of linear combinations (*scores*) among discriminant functions for that particular individual.

The risk manager can predetermine the predictor variables, or they can be selected using the iterative *discriminant analysis* or *step by step*.

The *linear discriminant analysis* operates on the same principle as the step-by-step *linear regression*: variables are added sequentially, in the model, until no further improvement is obtained in the discrimination (within the limits of stopping criterion). The *discriminant analysis* is often used in marketing to distinguish purchases of a new product through nonbuyers to identify different groups of response to a mail-order campaign: low, medium, and high. It is also used to develop models of *credit risk*. This method has *strengths* and *weaknesses*.

As *strengths*, we could say that this technique can separate and classify individuals into multiple groups. The idea of scoring an individual using a cut point (or *cutoff*) is peculiar of this methodology. It can be easily recognized as the right tool for *credit scoring*.

As *weaknesses*, this method assumes that predictor variables are normally distributed [0,1]; 0 meaning the average and 1 the standard

---

1. For the binary prediction, the formulas became into one single formula since the probability of association into one of the two groups, exclusive to one another, also reveals the probability of association in the other group.

deviation). This assumption is often violated in typical applications of scoring. Despite this predictive technique being robust in some ways with respect to minor violations of assumptions, the most serious violations cause frequently fallible estimates, or they do not inspire trust.

Another weakness is when some or all independent variables are highly correlated (i.e., in situations often called "multicollinearity"). The procedure could select a set of nonappropriate variables as if these were optimal. In fact, in situations of multicollinearity, the estimators of the regression coefficient (β_j) remarkably fluctuate from sample to sample.

2.2 Univariate Discriminant Analysis

Beaver (1966) used the univariate *discriminant analysis*, demonstrating that financial ratios can be used to predict insolvency of companies. From here, the studies on insolvency were successively improved and refined.

2.3 Multivariate Discriminant Analysis

Altman (1968) introduced the multivariate *discriminant analysis* model known as Z-score, and in a set of sixty-six companies, he managed to identify those who expressed a strong trend toward insolvency.

Later, Altman, Haldeman, and Narayanan (1977) developed a new model designated by Zeta™. Z-score and Zeta™ models were further referred to in other investigations, namely by Holmen (1988), Mosmann *et al.* (1998), Ooghe *et al.* (1999), Shumway (2001), Chava and Jarrow (2001), and Ooghe and Balcaen (2002).

At the culmination of the 1970s, models supported in the multivariate *discriminant analysis* reigned. However, some problems were identified in this statistical technique, which took the assumption of a normal distribution. Incidentally, Eisenbeis (1977) pointed out seven different types of problems: (1) the distribution of variables; (2) equality versus inequality of the dispersion of the groups; (3) the role of the weight of the individual variables; (4) issues arising from reducing the number of variables; (5) problems in defining groups (*discriminant analysis* assumed that the target research groups were discrete and identifiable); (6) inappropriate use of *ex-ante* probabilities in the classification of groups; and (7) classification problems in estimating error rates in the access to the performance of the model. These problems led to new investigations of other techniques.

According to Reis (2001, 201), "The discriminant analysis came up with the desire to statistically distinguish between two or more groups of individuals previously defined from characteristics known to all group members."

The process of granting credit leads to a choice between two actions: granting or denying credit to a new applicant.

Credit scoring tries to deal with this decision, finding out what would have been the best rule to apply, in a sample of candidates previously known. The advantage of doing so is to know the subsequent performance of these candidates. If there are only two possible actions, accept or reject, then there is no advantage in classifying this performance in more than two classes (*compliant* or *defaulting*). *Compliant* is any individual, defined from known characteristics, who will be granted the credit requested. *Defaulting* is the individual whose characteristics do not allow any financial institution to grant credit.

In the course of this work, we shall also use the terms "good credit" for compliant and "bad credit" for defaulting. In some financial institutions, 0 (bad) is considered failure to comply with several consecutive payments, while in other institutions, the criterion is the total amount of missing payments. First, these assumptions suffer from bias since the selected sample only concerns previously accepted candidates soon considered compliants, and there is not any information in a previous period about the performance of those candidates who have been refused credit.

Thus, the sample is only representative of those who were accepted (supposedly good), and it is not representative of the population (i.e., not including those who applied for a loan and who were considered, by their profile or behavior, rejected defaulters). According to Müller *et al.* (2002), "There is usually no information on the performance of rejected customers."

Hand and Henley (1993) concluded that the same cannot be exceeded, unless a special relationship can be assumed between the distributions of good and bad customers. This difficulty, according to the same researchers, can be partially solved: financial institutions that accept any candidate, for a certain period of time, will build a scorecard, a posteriori, based on a nonbiased sample data. This hypothesis is only possible in companies in which the method of risk analysis is the behavioral scoring.

From the analysis we have just carried out, we can accept that it will not be worth trying to identify the differences among the candidates in a given group when the decision of them belonging to this group is the sole responsibility of the lender.

Whatever the reasoning behind the decision to accept the candidate, the process is defined in the classification of applicants accepted into only two groups—good and bad—since the final decision will result in one of two actions: granting or refusing credit.

Suppose that a certain individual X_i was classified according to his/her characteristics—such as age, income, etc.—until the characteristic "p". In another way, let us assume that $X_i = (X_1, X_2, ..., X_p)$, in which the random variable "p" describes the available information on the individual X_i In this context, we shall use the words *"characteristic"* and *"variable"* as synonyms, the former used when you want to remember what kind of information is nominal and the latter when you want to emphasize the random nature of this information.

In credit-scoring terminology, the possible values or different responses of a *characteristic* are called *attributes*. For example, "single" is an *attribute* of the *marital-status characteristic*.

Financial institutions may require different attributes for the same characteristic in their application forms, also called accession proposals. We often confuse "characteristic" and "attribute." Characteristic is the *question* of the form, and attribute is its *answer*. For example: *Question*: In what kind of housing do you live? *Answer*: In a rented house. In this case, "housing" is the characteristic, and "rented" is the attribute.

Table 2. Example of various attributes of a characteristic

	Possible attributes for the characteristic HOUSING	
1	Own house free of mortgage	
2	Own house still mortgaged	
3	Rented unfurnished	X
4	Rented furnished	
5	Parents' house	
6	Home for young people	
7	Rented room	
8	Caravan	

It is assumed that, in filling out the application form for credit, the characteristics (questions) have a finite number of discrete attributes (answers), so the set of all attributes is finite. This corresponds to saying that there is only a finite number of ways to fill out that form.

2.4 Discriminant Function

The *discriminant analysis* is achieved according to one or more linear combinations of the independent variables X_i, or *candidate characteristics*). Each linear combination (Z_i) is a discriminant function:

$$Z_i = \alpha_0 + \beta_{i1}X_1 + \beta_{i2}X_2 + \ldots + \beta_{ip}X_p \qquad [1]$$

Wherein α_0 is a constant (independent from X_i), β_{ij} are parameters or weighting coefficients, and X_i are nonstandardized discriminant variables. Thus, we multiply each independent variable X_j by its corresponding parameter β_{ij}, and we add up these products to α_0, and the result obtained is the discriminant Z_i score for each individual candidate for credit. If this score is above a certain value (*cutoff*), the candidate for credit is accepted; if below the value, he/she is rejected. According to the criteria, $. \leq 0.05$ is rejected and > 0.05 is accepted.

Through the set of selected variables that allow discrimination, it is possible to classify new candidates whose grouping is initially unknown.

According to Reis (2001, 206), "*Discriminant analysis* can be understood as a system of scores that, to each individual, matches a score resulting from a weighted average of the values that, for him/her, take the independent variables."

To use the *discriminant analysis* in credit scoring, it is necessary to meet strict assumptions, namely that independent variables (characteristics of the candidate) are normally distributed and have the variance-covariance matrix equal in both groups, i.e., in good and bad candidates/users.

Chapter 3

Logistic Regression

3.1 Logistic-Regression Models (Logit)

In the 1980s, the focus of research moved to the *logistic-regression* models, also called *logit*.

Ohlson (1980) conducted the first study. Wiginton (1980) was one of the first researchers to publish the results on credit scoring using this technique.

Zavgren and Friedman (1988); Aziz and Lawnson (1989); Pearsons (1999); Wilson, Summers, and Hope (2000); Eklund, Larsen, and Behardsen (2001); Westgaard and Wijst (2001); Hayden (2002); Platt and Platt (2002); among other researchers applied *logistic regression*.

In statistics, the term *"regression"* means the functional dependence between two or more random variables corresponding mathematically to obtain a function that best represents the dependence between those variables.

The *logit* model was inserted in medical statistical terminology in 1944 by Berkson. *Logistic regression* compared with *discriminant analysis* has the advantage of not having to meet strict assumptions like the latter one—see Kaltofen, Möllenbeck, and Stein (2004); Ewert and Szczesny (2002); Jagtiani *et al.* (2000); Maddala (1983); Ohlson (1980); Press and Wilson (1978); and Martin (1977).

In scoring application, we do not intend to determine a large number of values for the dependent variable using, in turn, binary variables that take the values 0 or 1. What the linear regression model does is estimate the probability of the event not failing. Although linear regression is sometimes used to estimate scoring models, *logistic regression* is generally preferred because it is especially adaptable to cases in which there is a binary-dependent variable or a dummy variable. A problem with the use of linear regression is that it can produce a higher probability than 1 and less than 0, which is absurd.

The *logistic model* prevents that absurdity because it responds with inequalities of the event, rather than probabilities.

This model is based on the natural Neper's logarithm, or *(e)*,[2] avoiding negative probabilities. Thus, in the *logistic-regression* model, the coefficients of the independent or explanatory variables are linearly related, not only with Y, as in the case of linear regression, but also with the natural logarithm of the probability of a Y, as we shall see below.

3.2 Logistic Function

Logistic-regression analysis is a statistical technique constituting a mathematical model that allows predicting values, with dummy-dependent variable. The popularity of *logistic regression* is based on the *logistic function* that describes the mathematical form in which the *logistic model* is based. This feature translates into the equation:

$$f(z) = \frac{1}{1+e^{-z}}$$

[2]

To plot the graph of the logistic function, it will be given values to z to obtain $f(z)$.

---

3. A natural logarithm or logarithm exponent, the base is represented by *e* and is called Neper's number. It is an irrational number whose value is approximately 2.718282 and can be obtained by calculating the limit of the real sucession of general-term converges.

Table 3. Z data to plot f(Z)

Z	f(Z)
-5	0.0066928509
-4	0.0179862100
-3	0.0474258732
-2	0.1192029220
-1	0.2689414214
0	0.5000000000
1	0.7310585786
2	0.8807970780
3	0.9525741268
4	0.9820137900
5	0.9933071491

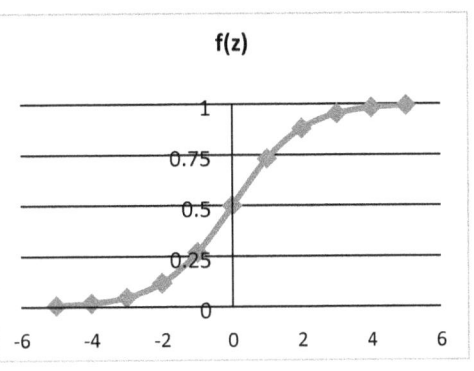

Figure 2. Logistic function graph.

The model is designed to predict the probability of default of any candidate for credit, whose probability is always between 0 and 1.

Thus, the *logistic model* may never get a possibility of risk higher than 100 percent or lower than 0 percent. This finding is not always true for other models, which is why the *logistic model* is usually the first choice when you want to determine the probability of default.

Another reason why the *logistic model* is so popular comes from the graph of the logistic function. As illustrated in Figure 2, if we start by giving values to $z = -\infty$, the value of $f(z)$ is approximately 0, $[f(z) \approx 0]$, and as $f(z)$ moves to the right, it increases rapidly toward 1, and finally it slowly approaches 1 without ever reaching it. The plotting result of the function is an elongated "S".

The variable z is the representation of an *index* that combines the contributions of several risk factors, and $f(z)$ represents the probability of default risk.

The *logistic model* is popular because the *logistic function*, on which the model is based, enables the following: the default probability is between 0 and 1, and the shape of an elongated "S" describes the combined effect of several risk factors on the risk of default.

3.3 Logistic Model

From the *logistic function*, let us focus on the model, which is our first goal. To obtain the *logistic model* from the *logistic function*, we translate "z" as a linear sum of α plus β_1 times X_1, plus β_2 times X_2, plus β_3 times X_3, ... , plus β_k times X_k, where X_s are the independent variables for risk analysis, and α and β_j are constants that represent unknown parameters:

$$z = \alpha + \beta_1 X_1 + \beta_2 X_2 + \ldots + \beta_k X_k \qquad [3]$$

Where:

α- is the parameter of the model called *constant* (because it does not depend on X);

β_j are the parameters of the model called *coefficients* of the variables X_j; and

X_j are the independent variables.

Then Z is an *index* that combines the X_s. Replacing z in the *logistic function* [2], we obtain:

$$f(z) = \frac{1}{1 + e^{-(\alpha + \beta_1 X_1 + \beta_2 X_2 + \ldots + \beta_k X_k)}}$$

$$f(z) = \frac{1}{1 + e^{-(\alpha + \sum \beta_i X_i)}}$$

[4]

3.4 Transforming Probabilities into Odds

Now let us introduce the ratio between the probability that an event occurs and the probability it does not occur. In other words, we calculate a ratio between the probability the default occurs and the probability the default does not occur. This ratio is designated by *odds*.

"Odds" is a numerical expression used in statistics, horse-race betting, and some games to translate the probability of a given event occurring. That is, the probability of occurrence in relation to the probability of nonoccurrence.

For example, if the probability of a customer defaulting is 70 percent, then the probability of not defaulting is 30 percent.

The ratio between these two probabilities determines *odds*, or 2.33. The number 2.33 means there are 2.33 favorable results in 3.33 possible cases, such as where the event has not taken place once. If we divide 2.33 (number of favorable cases) by 3.33 (number of possible cases), we get the figure of 70 percent. We can say probability is 2.33 to 1 (or 2.33:1).

Represented by P_i, the probability of an event occurs; the probability it does not occur is $1 - P_i$.

$$Odds = \frac{P_i}{1 - P_i}$$

[5]

3.5 Natural Logarithm of Odds

The transformation of probabilities into natural logarithms *(ln)* involves two steps.

The first step was explained in section 3.4, and it consisted of finding the ratio between P_i and $1 - P_i$. The second step is to determine the natural logarithm of *odds*.

Step 1:
$$Odds = \frac{P_i}{1 - P_i}$$

Step 2:
$$\ln odds = \ln \frac{P_i}{1-P_i}$$
[6]

The expression "logged odds" (or "logit") is used as an abbreviation of "ln odds."

In the example given above, if the default probability is 70 percent, the *odds* value will be 2.33, and its *logit* will be 0.847.

Although the formula used to transform probabilities into *logits* is direct, it requires some explanation to justify its usefulness. That formula describes the relationship between independent variables and a probability distribution defined by the dichotomous-dependent variable.

3.6 Meaning of Odds

The transformation of probabilities into *odds* and the application of the natural logarithm into *odds* result in *logged odds* (or *logit*). The probabilities range from 0 (lower limit) to 1 (upper limit). The *odds* are expressed by a ratio between the probability that an event occurs and the probability it does not occur, i.e., $=\frac{P_i}{1-P_i}$. The probabilities and the *odds* have 0 as a lower limit; that is when $P_i = 0$ will be $odds = \frac{0}{1-0} = 0$.

Unlike the probability, *odds* do not have an upper limit or ceiling. As the probability is closer to 1, the numerator of the *odds* (P_i) becomes increasingly larger (0,9999...9) in relation to the denominator ($1 - P_i$), and the *odds* become increasingly very large numbers. The *odds* increase much when the probabilities change only slightly near its upper border (see table 4).

For example, probabilities of 0.99, 0.999, 0.9999, 0.99999, and so on result in *odds* 99; 999; 9,999; 99,999; etc. Small changes in probabilities result in enormous changes in *odds,* and they show that odds increase toward positive infinite $+\infty$ as probabilities approach 1.

	Lower limit	Upper limit
Probabilities	0	1
Odds	0	$+\infty$

To illustrate the relationship between probabilities and *odds*, see the values in table 4.

Table 4. Quantitative relationship between probabilities and respective *odds*

P_i	0.01	0.1	0.2	0.3	0.4	0.5	0.6	0.7	0.8	0.9	0.99	0.999	...	0.99999	$P_i \rightarrow 1$
$1 - P_i$	0.99	0.9	0.8	0.7	0.6	0.5	0.4	0.3	0.2	0.1	0.01	0.001	...	0.00001	$1 - P_i \rightarrow 0$
odds	0.01	0.111	0.25	0.429	0.667	1	1.5	2.33	4	9	99	999	...	99999	$\dfrac{\lim_{P_i \rightarrow 1} P_i}{\lim_{1-P_i \rightarrow 0} 1-P_i} =$

When probability is equal to 0.5, *odds* are equal to 1. Probabilities increase toward 1, while *odds* tend to very large numbers.

By manipulating the formula for the *odds*, we shall better understand their relationship with *probabilities*. Beginning with the definition of *odds* (O_i) as the ratio between the probability (P_i) on 1 minus the probability ($1 - P_i$), we can express with a simple algebraic calculation the probability in terms of *odds* (O_i):

$$O_i = \frac{P_i}{1 - P_i}$$
$$O_i - O_i P_i = P_i$$
$$O_i = P_i + O_i P_i$$

$$O_i = P_i(1 + O_i)$$

$$P_i = \frac{O_i}{1 + O_i}$$

[7]

The probability (P_i) is equal to the ratio between *odds* (O_i) and 1 plus *odds* ($1 + O_i$).

As exemplified above when referring to the probability of defaulting, 70 percent was obtained by dividing 2.33/(1+2.33).

Supported in this formula, the probability will never be equal to or exceed the unit. It does not matter how large the *odds* are into the numerator, as the probability P_i will always be between 0 and 1.

The utility of *odds* will be demonstrated later in the interpretation of coefficients, but the creation of *odds* represents the first step of the *logit* transformation.

3.7 Logged Odds (or Logit)

Taking the natural logarithm of the *odds* (*logit*), we eliminate the lower limit of *odds* (=0); changing probabilities into *odds* eliminates the upper limit of probabilities (=1).

Thus:

log *odds* above 0 but below 1 produce negative numbers;
log *odds* equal to 1 produce 0; and
log *odds* above 1 produce positive numbers.

1 > log *odds* > 0	⟹ Negative numbers	⟹	− ∞
log *odds* = 1	⟹ 0		
log *odds* > 1	⟹ Positive numbers	⟹	

3.8 Logit Properties

First property: *logit*, contrary to probability, has no upper or lower limit.

Odds eliminate the upper limit of probabilities. That is, the upper limit of probabilities ($= 1$) when *odds* are applied, tends to $+\infty$.

Logged *odds* (the natural logarithms of *odds*) eliminate the lower limit of the probabilities, i.e., the lower limit of the probability ($= 0$) when in its neighborhood (e.g., 0.00000000...01) the *logit* is applied, tends to $-\infty$.

Making $P_i = 1$, *logit* results are indefinite because *odds* $\frac{1}{0}$ does not exist (it is impossible). Once the probability is closer to 1, *logit* moves toward $+\infty$.

If $P_i = 0$, *logit* is also indefinite because logarithm of *odds* $\frac{0}{1}$ does not exist. As the probability is increasingly closer to 0, *logit* moves toward $-\infty$. Thus, *logits* range from minus infinity $-\infty$ to plus infinity $+\infty$. The problem of an upper limit and a lower limit on probabilities (or a lower limit of *odds*) ceases.

Second property: *logit* transformation is symmetrical, related to the midpoint of the probability (0.5). When $P_i = 0.5 \Rightarrow logit = 0$ (i.e. $\frac{0.5}{0.5} = 1$, $\Rightarrow \ln 1 = 0$)

Probabilities below 0.5 result in negative *logit* because *odds* drop below 1 and above 0 (P_i is less than $1 - P_i$).

Probabilities $= 0.5$ result in $logit = 0$, since

$$O_i = \frac{P_i}{1 - P_i} = \frac{0.5}{1 - 0.5} = \frac{0.5}{0.5} = 1, \Rightarrow \ln 1 = 0.$$

Probabilities above 0.5 result in positive *logit* because *odds* exceed 1 (P_i is greater than $1 - P_1$).

Furthermore, the probabilities of the same distance above and below 0.5 (i.e. 0.6, and 0.4, or 0.7 and 0.3, or 0.8 and 0.2) have the same *logit* but opposite signals (*logits* for the abovementioned probabilities are, respectively, 0.405 and -0.405; 0.847 and -0.847; 1.386 and -1.386).

P_i	logit
0.1	-2.197
0.2	-1.386
0.3	-0.847
0.4	-0.405
0.5	0
0.6	0.405
0.7	0.847
0.8	1.386
0.9	2.197

The distance of *logit* from 0 reflects the distance of the probability from 0.5 (again, *logits* do not have limits as the probabilities).

Third property: the same change in the probabilities cause different changes in *logits*. The principle is simple: as P_i comes closer to 0 and 1, the same change in the probability causes a bigger change in logged *odds*, as we can see in table 5.

Table 5. The same change in probabilities (of 0.1) cause different changes in *legit*

P_i	0.1	0.2	0.3	0.4	0.5	0.6	0.7	0.8	0.9
$1-P_i$	0.9	0.8	0.7	0.6	0.5	0.4	0.3	0.2	0.1
Odds	0.111	0.25	0.429	0.667	1	1.5	2.33	4	9
logit	-2.197	-1.386	-0.847	-0.405	0	0.405	0.847	1.386	2.197

An increase in the probabilities of 0.1 (going from 0.5 to 0.6, or from 0.5 to 0.4) results in a change in the *logit* of 0.405. The same increase in probabilities of 0.1 (going from 0.8 to 0.9 or 0.2 to 0.1) results in a change (a difference) in the *logit* of 0.811 (2.197 – 1.386).

The general principle is that small differences in probabilities cause a greater increase in the differences of *logits* when the probabilities are close to the limits 0 and 1.

3.9 Obtaining Probabilities through Logits

The linear relationship between the independent variables and dependent-variable *logit* implies nonlinear relationships with probabilities. The linear relation of X to the predicted *logit* is translated as:

$$\ln\left(\frac{P_i}{1-P_i}\right) = \alpha + \beta_i X_i \qquad [8]$$

To express probabilities instead of *logit* as a function of X, we must take each side of the equation as an exponent "e", thus:

$$e^{\ln\left(\frac{P_i}{1-P_i}\right)} = e^{\alpha + \beta_i X_i} \qquad [9]$$

Once $e^{\ln X} = X$, it will become:

$$\frac{P_i}{1-P_i} = e^{\alpha + \beta_i X_i} \qquad [10]$$

$$\frac{P_i}{1-P_i} = e^{\alpha} \times e^{\beta_i X_i} \qquad [11]$$

Solving the equation to P_i:

$$P_i = (1 - P_i) \times e^{\alpha} \times e^{\beta_i X_i}$$
$$P_i = e^{\alpha} \times e^{\beta_i X_i} - (P_i \times e^{\alpha} \times e^{\beta_i X_i})$$
$$P_i + \left(P_i \times e^{\alpha} \times e^{\beta_i X_i}\right) = e^{\alpha} \times e^{\beta_i X_i}$$
$$P_i\left(1 + e^{\alpha} \times e^{\beta_i X_i}\right) = e^{\alpha} \times e^{\beta_i X_i}$$

$$P_i = \frac{e^\alpha \times e^{\beta_i X_i}}{1 + e^\alpha \times e^{\beta_i X_i}}$$

$$P_i = \frac{e^{\alpha + \beta_i X_i}}{1 + e^{\alpha + \beta_i X_i}}$$

[12]

Once $logit\ Z$ is equal to $\alpha + \beta_i X_i$, it will be possible to replace it in the formula, obtaining:

$$P_i = \frac{e^z}{1 + e^z}$$

[13]

Recall that *logit* or logged *odds* are abbreviations or simplifications of ln *odds*, so the above equation could also be written as:

$$P_i = \frac{e^{\ln odds}}{1 + e^{\ln odds}}$$

But because the Neper's number (e) raised to the natural logarithm of a number is equal to that same number, it will be:

$$P_i = \frac{odds}{1 + odds}$$

Representing *odds* by O_i and replacing it in the previous formula:

$$P_i = \frac{O_i}{1 + O_i}$$

Expression already previously found [7]

3.10 An Alternative Formula to Calculate Probability

The formula for probability P_i, according to the independent variables and parameters (α, β_i) is:

$$P_i = \frac{e^{\alpha + \beta_i X_i}}{1 + e^{\alpha + \beta_i X_i}}$$

Dividing the numerator and the denominator of the fraction by the numerator:

$$P_i = \frac{1}{\dfrac{1}{e^{\alpha + \beta_i X_i}} + \dfrac{e^{\alpha + \beta_i X_i}}{e^{\alpha + \beta_i X_i}}}$$

$$P_i = \frac{1}{\dfrac{1}{e^{\alpha + \beta_i X_i}} + 1}$$

$$P_i = \frac{1}{e^{-(\alpha + \beta_i X_i)} + 1}$$

But $z = \alpha + \beta_i X_i$

$$P_i = \frac{1}{e^{-z} + 1}$$

[14]

Chapter 4

General Procedure in Parameters Estimation

4.1 Introduction

Now that you have a statistical model (*logistic model*) to determine the dichotomous-dependent variable, the next step is to use data from a sample to estimate the model parameters. The sample that was used consisted of 1,600 good customers and 1,600 bad customers whose full development is the subject of *chapter 8*.

In this chapter, the general purpose of parameter estimation will be explained through the *maximum-likelihood method,* including a discussion of the *Likelihood Function* $LF(\theta)$ and how these are maximized $LF(\theta)_{Max}$.

4.2 Maximum-Likelihood Method

The good use of data in statistical methods depends on its type, its cleaning, and treatment to provide reliable results. If grouped data, there are three available methods: the method of least squares; the method of weighted least squares; and the method of *maximum likelihood*.

The *maximum-likelihood method* is used to estimate the parameters of a statistical model from a data set. This is a more suitable method for *logistic regression* to estimate the *logistic model* for combined data and the only method generally used for data individual level.

It is through these data of individual nature (age, gender, occupation, marital status, annual income, etc.), properly weighted, that you get the dichotomous-dependent variable (0 or 1) whose meaning, here we recall, is to not grant credit or grant credit.

As mentioned above, the estimation of parameters by *maximum-likelihood method* is one of several approaches that have been developed to estimate parameters in a mathematical model representing the estimation by the *least-squares method,* another well-known and very popular approach.

Estimation by *maximum-likelihood* and *least-squares* methods are different approaches, which give the same results for the classical linear regression when the dependent variable is assumed to be normally distributed [0;1].

For many years, the *maximum-likelihood* estimation was not used because there were no computer resources available by software that could perform highly complex and time-consuming calculations. However, programs that allow the calculation of the *maximum-likelihood* function (LF_{Max}) are now widely spread.

When comparing *least-squares* and *maximum-likelihood* methods, the latter has the advantage that it can be applied in the estimation of complex nonlinear model parameters and in linear models.

In particular, because the *logistic model* is a nonlinear model, *maximum likelihood* is the preferred estimation method for *logistic regression*.

Until there were computer programs allowing computational calculation for estimation by the *maximum-likelihood* method, *discriminant analysis* was used to estimate *logistic model* parameters.

This technique is essentially an approach by the least-squares method. To perform statistical inference of the model parameters, a verification of the normal restrictive assumptions is required in the logistic function–independent variables.

In particular, if any of the independent variables is dichotomous (e.g., gender) or categorical, then the method of discriminating function tends to produce biased results, usually giving very high *odds* ratios.

The *maximum-likelihood* estimation, on the other hand, does not require any restriction of any kind of the independent variable characteristics. Thus, when using *maximum-likelihood* estimation, independent variables can be categorical (binary, ordinal, nominal, and fictitious) and numerical (continuous, discrete, and cardinal).

Maximizing the likelihood (probability) is used to estimate parameters β_1 up to β_k. These parameter estimates measure the rate of change of the *logit* for a unit change in the input variable (adjusted for the other entries). This means that they are, in fact, the slope of the regression line between the result (target) and its respective input variables x_1 up to x_k.

Parameters are dependent on the input unit (i.e., a percentage compared with the result), and they need to be standardized to facilitate the analysis. One possible way is to go over the input units together and develop the regression not due to the input but due to the *weight of evidence* $\left(WOE = \ln\dfrac{\%Good}{\%Bad}\right)$ of each group created in the previous phase.

Regression needs to have a target and a series of inputs. These can have various forms. The most common way is to use original inputs for numerical variables and to create fictitious variables (dummies) for categorical data. Standardized estimates are then used in the analysis to neutralize the effects of the input variable units. This procedure is not, however, relevant when the variables are combined for the development of scorecards.

In the case of the scorecard-grouped variables, inputs can be aligned with the numerical average of each group of variables, such as the average age of each group, weighted averages, or fictitious averages for nominal or categorical groups (e.g., young people, adults, and seniors).

By using dummy variables for categorical variables, some problems have arisen, because it is assumed that the difference between a categorical variable group and the next group is the same. The best way to live with grouped variables is to use the WOE of each group as an input. This not only solves the problems of different input units, it also considers the exact trend and the scale or range of the ratio from one group to the next one. It also helps to develop scorecards while preserving each individual feature of the analysis. Additionally, if the grouping is well done, it will ensure that the points allocation in each group during the scheduling phase of the scorecard is logical and represents the difference in the relations between groups.

4.3 Step-by-Step Logistic-Regression Techniques

4.3.1 Forward Selection

First, we should select the best characteristic based on its predictive strength. Then we add the following characteristics to the template to create the best two, three, four, and so on characteristics until there are no more characteristics with a *p-value* lower than a certain significance level (e.g. 0.05) or a value of univariate chi-square above a certain level. This method is efficient, but it may be weakened if characteristics are too highly correlated.

4.3.2 Backward Elimination

This method is the reverse of the previous technique. It starts with all the characteristics in the model, and in sequential order, those considered of lower significance are eliminated until all remaining ones present a *p-value* of a certain level (e.g., 0.01). This method allows the variables of lower significance to have a higher probability of entering the model.

4.3.3 Combination of Previous Techniques (Stepwise)

This technique uses addition and removal of characteristics dynamically through the scorecard for each stage until the best match is found. A user can establish required minimum *p-values* necessary to add to or keep in the model.

$$Z_i = \alpha + \beta_1 x_{i1} + \beta_2 x_{i2} + \dots + \beta_k x_{ik} \qquad [15]$$

$$p_i = \frac{1}{1 + e^{-(\alpha + \beta_1 x_{i1} + \beta_2 x_{i2} + \ldots + \beta_k x_{ik})}}$$

[16]

Figure 3. *Logit* model for a single explanatory variable

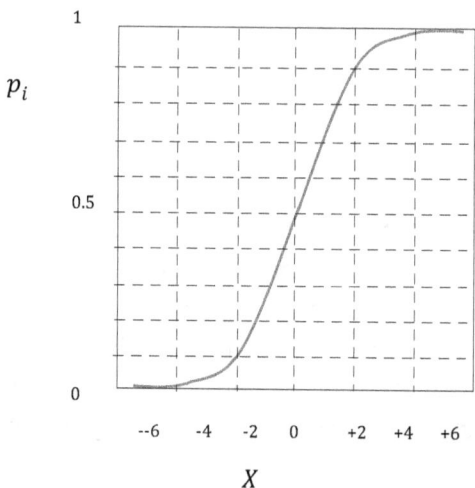

If we have a single variable x with $\alpha = 0$ and $\beta = 1$, the equation (figure 3) takes a curve symmetrically by a serpentine "S", where $p_i \in\,]0;1[$ for any "X".

This regression adopts the *maximum-likelihood* method to find the most likely estimates for coefficients of independent variables. The *logistic model* also takes the form of conditional probability, according to Hair et al. (1988):

$$p_i = Pr(Y_i = 1|X = \frac{e^{\alpha + \beta_1 X_{i1} + \ldots + \beta_k X_{ik}}}{1 + e^{\alpha + \beta_1 X_{i1} + \ldots + \beta_k X_{ik}}}$$

[17]

Logistic regression is a common technique used in the development of scorecards for most applications of financial institutions, where the predictive variable is categorical.

Where the predictor is continuous, we use linear regression. *Logistic regression* uses a set of predictive characteristics to predict the probability of a particular outcome.

Parametric statistical methods, which we have introduced (*discriminant analysis* and *logistic regression*), have the disadvantage that their applications can be seriously affected, in their predictive techniques, by extreme values (*outliers*) and default data (*missing data*), according to Schewe and Lekert (2000) and Espahbodi et al. (2003).

According to Frydman, Altman, and Kao (1985), additional statistical problems may arise, caused by violation of assumptions of normality and independence, reduction of the dimensionality of variables, and interpretation of their relative importance, making the accuracy of the results questionable.

4.4 Classification of Variable Characteristics

The classification of a variable is not always intuitive and immediate, allowing for some distortions in the model estimation if that classification is not acceptable. In this sense, let's recall some concepts.

Categorical variables are those grouped by a common quality, such as gender (male or female) or color (red, yellow, blue, green, etc.).

Binary categorical variables are those with only two possible categories, also called dichotomous: male/female, true/false, correct/incorrect, good/bad, heads/tails, present/absent, grant credit/refuse credit, 1/0, etc.

Ordinal categorical variables are those that indicate a relative position in a sequence associated with degrees of evaluation, such as excellent, very good, good, fair, poor, bad, or very bad.

Nominal categorical variables are those represented by different categories, such as names or codes (letters and numbers, zip codes, etc.), and not indicating any relationship or priority order.

Numerical variables are those established by numbers that can be used in mathematical calculations.

Continuous numerical variables are those established in uninterrupted series with an infinite number of possible values. These variables are associated with real numbers and especially with measures, such as temperature, weight, distance, and time.

Discrete numerical variables are distinct and separate and not continuous. They are associated with integers presented in sequence.

Discrete numerical cardinal variables specifically refer to counts within a set.

4.5 Estimation by Maximum Likelihood vs. Discriminant Analysis

Estimation by *maximum likelihood* is preferable to *discriminant analysis* function for adjustment of the *logistic model*. Basic principle of *maximum likelihood* is to choose estimate values of parameters that, if true, will maximize the probability of verifying what we came to observe.

There are two steps to do that: (1) write an expression for the probability of data as a function of the unknown parameters and (2) find the values of unknown parameters that make the value of this expression as large as possible (maximization).

The first step is known as a builder of the *likelihood function*. To perform this step, you must specify a model equivalent to choosing a probability distribution for the dependent variable in the *logistic model*, choosing a functional form related to the parameters of this distribution for values of the explanatory variables.

In the case of the *logistic model* (*logit*), the presented dichotomous-dependent variable has a binomial distribution, where P_i

is the probability that depends on the explanatory variables according to the *logit* model expressed by the equation:

$$\ln\left(\frac{P_i}{1 - P_i}\right) = \alpha + \beta_1 X_1 + \beta_2 X_2 + \ldots + \beta_k X_k$$

[18]

The second step (maximization) requires the application of an iterative numerical method, which means the use of a repetitive process by successive approximations.

4.6 Likelihood Function $LF(\theta)$ and Its Use in the Procedure of Maximum Likelihood (LF_{Max})

To describe the procedure of *maximum likelihood*, we introduce the *likelihood function* (LF). This is a function of unknown parameters, and it may be alternatively provided by $LF(\theta)$ where θ is the set of unknown parameters that will be estimated by the model.

$$LF = LF(\theta) = Likelihood\ Function$$

In matrix language, the (θ) set is called vector. Vector components are the individual parameters to be estimated in the model and represented by $\theta_1, \theta_2, \ldots, \theta_q$ being q the number of individual components:

$$\theta = (\theta_1, \theta_2, \ldots, \theta_q)$$

Estimation by *maximum likelihood* allows us to find the estimates of model parameters that are more likely to replicate the observation pattern in the sample data. To illustrate the *maximum-likelihood* precept, consider tossing a coin fifteen times, resulting in nine heads-up results.

According to binomial Bernoulli distribution:

$$P(x) = \binom{n}{x} p^x . q^{n-x}$$

[19]

Where "x" represents the number of heads, "n" the number of coin tosses, "p" the probability of landing heads up, and "q" the probability of landing on tails:

$$P(9) = \binom{15}{9} p^9 . q^{15-9}$$

But $q = 1 - p$

$$P(9) = \frac{15!}{(15-9)! \times 9!} p^9 . (1-p)^{15-9}$$

$$P(9) = \frac{15!}{6! \times 9!} p^9 . (1-p)^6$$

"p" represents a probability equal to P_i and equal to the probability of a head and $1 - P_i$ the probability of tails, the probability to have nine heads and six tails is equal to:

$$P(9h\ hHeads,\ 6\ Tails) = \frac{15!}{6! \times 9!} \times [P_i^9 \times (1 - P_i)^6] = 5005 \times [P_i^9 \times (1 - P_i)^6]$$

We shall assume, a priori, that with a fair coin, the P_i of getting heads or tails would be equiprobable, i.e., .0.5 (50 percent).

If P_i is unknown, one needs to assess the trustworthiness of the coin or, put another way, decipher the probabilistic trend of the coin through the translation of an expression that as closely as possible approximates the results that will be observed.

However, the question that arises now is: how can P_i be estimated by the results observed in nine heads out of the fifteen times the coin was tossed? The estimate by *maximum likelihood* chooses P_i that makes the likelihood of obtaining the observed result as close to reality as possible.

For this, we have to find the estimated P_i by *maximum likelihood*. Let us focus on the expression $[P_i^9 \times (1 - P_i)^6]$ of the formula presented for solving the problem. That formula expresses the probability of obtaining nine heads as a function of various values of P_i. Entering the possible values of P_i into likelihood function, we obtain the results in table 6:

Table 6. Results of the likelihood function, depending on the different probabilities of P_i

P_i	$P_i^9 \times (1 - P_i)^6$
	Likelihood function
0.1	0.0000000005314
0.2	0.0000001342177
0.3	0.0000023156853
0.4	0.0000122305905
0.5	0.0000305175781
0.6	0.0000412782428
0.7	0.0000294177795
0.8	0.0000085899346
0.9	0.0000003874205

$P(9\ heads,\ 6\ tails) = 5005 \times 0{,}0000412782428 = 0{,}206598 \cong 21\%$

The *maximum* value found arises when $P_i = 0.6$. Further confirmations may be made to the probability by using the same formula when P_i varies between 0.55 and 0.63, confirming that $P_i = 0.6$ is the one that produces the maximum probability.

Table 7. Results of the *likelihood function* for values of between 0.55 e 0.63, confirming that the highest value for the *likelihood function* is to $P_i = 0.6$.

P_i	$P_i^9 \times (1 - P_i)^6$
0.55	0.0000382418847
0.56	0.0000393014254
0.57	0.0000401498969
0.58	0.0000407706546
0.59	0.0000411501332
0.6	0.0000412782428
0.61	0.0000411487036
0.62	0.0000407593064
0.63	0.0000401120899

Given the presented data, the estimate of most likely P_i or *maximum likelihood* is 0.6. Thus, we take the value that reveals the highest probability of producing the actual observations as the parameter estimate for P_i..

For *logistic regression*, the procedure begins with $Y = 1$ for the probability of observing the occurrences pattern and $Y = 0$ for the probability of not observing that pattern.

The expression is:

$$LF(\theta) = P_i^{Y_i} \times (1 - P_i)^{1 - Y_i}$$

[20]

called *likelihood function* depends on unknown parameters of the *logistic regression*.

As in the coin toss example, the *maximum-likelihood* estimation will find the model parameters, which will produce the maximum value for the likelihood function. That expression, thus, identifies the estimates for the model parameters, which are the most likely to fit the pattern of recorded observations in the sample data.

The *maximum-likelihood* function (LF_{Max}) in *logistic regression* is similar to the previous one:

$$LF_{Max} = \prod \left\{ P_i^{Y_i} \times (1 - P_i)^{1-Y_i} \right\} \quad [21]$$

Where $LF(\theta)$ is the likelihood function, Y_i is the observed value of the dichotomous-dependent variable (0 or 1) for case (individual) i, and P_i is the predicted probability for case i. Remember that P_i values come from the *logistic-regression* model and $P_i = \dfrac{1}{(1+e^{-z})}$ [14], where Z is equal to logged *odds* (*logit*) determined by unknown β coefficients and independent variables. The multiplicand ($\prod$) means that the function multiplies the values for each case. The key is to identify the values of β that produce values of Z and P_i that maximize $LF(\theta)$.

See how the formula reacts to a case where $Y_i = 1$. The formula is reduced to P_i:

$$LF(\theta) = \left\{ P_i^{Y_i} \times (1 - P_i)^{1-Y_i} \right\}$$
$$LF(\theta) = \left\{ P_i^{1} \times (1 - P_i)^{1-1} \right\}$$
$$LF(\theta) = \left\{ P_i \times (1 - P_i)^{0} \right\}$$
$$LF(\theta) = \left\{ P_i \times 1 \right\}$$
$$LF(\theta) = P_i$$

So when $Y_i = 1$ (the probability of observing the occurrences pattern), the value for a case i is equal to its estimated probability. If based on the coefficients of the model, the case has a high probability of observing the pattern of an event when $Y_i = 1$.

For a case in which $Y_i = 0$, the formula is reduced to $1 - P_i$:

$$LF(\theta) = \left\{ P_i^{Y_i} \times (1 - P_i)^{1-Y_i} \right\}$$

$$LF(\theta) = \{P_i^0 \times (1 - P_i)^1\}$$
$$LF(\theta) = \{1 \times (1 - P_i)^1\}$$

$$LF(\theta) = 1 - P_i$$

Thus, we have:
$$y_i = 1 \ : \ LF(\theta) = P_i$$

$$y_i = 0 \ : \ LF(\theta) = 1 - P_i$$

When $Y_i = 0$, the individual "i" has a low probability of occurring based on the model coefficients (i.e., if $P_i = 0.1$, then $1 - P_i = 0.9$.

Take, for example, four cases. Two candidates for credit have values of 1 (good) and the other two have values of 0 (bad). Assume that the estimated coefficients of the combination (by multiplication) with the values of the independent variables produced the estimated probabilities for each of the four cases, as shown in table 8.

Table 8. Example of four candidates for credit—two good and two bad—and their estimated probabilities

	Y_i	P_i	$P_i^{Y_i}$	$(1-P_i)^{1-Y_i}$	$P_i^{Y_i} \times (1-P_i)^{1-Y_i}$
					Likelihood function (LF)
Good	1	0.9	0.9	1	0.9
	1	0.8	0.8	1	0.8
Bad	0	0.2	1	0.8	0.8
	0	0.1	1	0.9	0.9
					$\Pi = 0.5184$

$$LF_{Max} = \prod = 0.9 \times 0.8 \times 0.8 \times 0.9 = 0.5184$$

For each case shown in table 8, the $LF(\theta)$ final value denotes that the observation probability of approaching the standard of occurrences is high.

Comparing these results with another set of estimated parameters, in combination (by multiplication) with the values of X (independent variables), produced estimated probabilities and different results, as shown in table 9:

Table 9. Example of four candidates for credit—two good and two bad—and their estimated probabilities

	Y_i	P_i	$P_i^{Y_i}$	$(1-P_i)^{1-Y_i}$	$P_i^{Y_i} \times (1-P_i)^{1-Y_i}$ Likelihood function (LF)
Good	1	0.1	0.1	1	0.1
	1	0.2	0.2	1	0.2
Bad	0	0.8	1	0.2	0.2
	0	0.9	1	0.1	0.1
					$\Pi = 0.0004$

$$LF_{Max} = \prod = 0.1 \times 0.2 \times 0.2 \times 0.1 = 0.0004$$

In the example in table 9, the estimated coefficients are worst by producing Y_i values, and the values of the respective probabilities are lower.

Given a set of estimates for the model parameters, the *maximum-likelihood* function (LF_{Max}) returns a probability for each case of sample values actually observed.

In multiplying these probabilities, we obtain an abbreviated indication of all cases of probabilities, which are produced by a set of parameters in the current values. Multiplying probabilities means that the final product cannot exceed 1 or be lower than 0.

The probability of the first set of parameters (table 8) is equal to the multiplicand:

$$\prod = 0.9 \times 0.8 \times 0.8 \times 0.9 = 0.5184$$

The probability of the second set of parameters (table 9) is equal to the multiplicand:

$$\prod = 0.1 \times 0.2 \times 0.2 \times 0.1 = 0.0004$$

Thus, it has been shown by single numbers (0.5184 and 0.0004) the results given in a more detailed calculations as illustrated in tables 8 and 9.

The hypothetical parameters considered in the first example showed a higher value for $LF(\theta)$ of 0.5184 than for those of the second example of 0.0004, and these parameters will approach the results of the logistic function to the observed data when multiplied by their respective independent variables.

4.7 Log-Likelihood Function (LLF)

As we have seen in tables 8 and 9 in section 4.6, the multiplications of probabilities lead us to very small numbers. This is what we have seen in the given example for the calculation of the probability of the second example, in which the value was 0.0004.

The way to overcome this problem is to transform the result of the *maximum-likelihood* function (LF_{Max}) by multiplying by the natural logarithm. The new function, thus, obtained is called *log-likelihood*.

(LLF – Logarithm of Likelihood Function)

Before proceeding to the calculations, just remember two more properties of logarithms for better understanding the following developments:

Logarithm of the product:

$\ln(a \times b) = \ln a + \ln b$

Logarithm of power:

$\ln(a^x) = x \times \ln a$

The *log-likelihood function* sums the original multiplicative terms. Taking the natural logarithm of both sides of the equation [20], we obtain the log-likelihood function:

$$\ln LF = \ln \left\{ P_i^{Y_i} \times (1 - P_i)^{1-Y_i} \right\}$$

$$\ln LF = \sum \left\{ [Y_i \times \ln P_i] + [(1 - Y_i)\ln(1 - P_i)] \right\} \quad [22]$$

If *likelihood function* varies between 0 and 1, the *log-likelihood function* varies from $-\infty$ up to 0 (the natural logarithm of 1 is equal to 0) and the log of 0 is undefined, but in probabilities near 0, the natural logarithm becomes a negative number increasing more and more, tending to $-\infty$.

The closer the value of the probability is to 1, the closest the *log likelihood* is from 0, and the greater the probability of the parameters producing the observed data.

The further the negative value is from 0, the lower the probability of the parameters producing the observed data.

To illustrate the *log-likelihood function*, we will use the example previously given.

Table 10. Example of *LLF* calculation with *low*-probability values of bad

Y_i	P_i	$Y_i \times \ln P_i$	$(1-Y_i)\ln(1-P_i)$	$\{[Y_i \times \ln P_i] + [(1-Y_i)\ln(1-P_i)]\}$
				Log-likelihood function
1	0.9	-0.10536	0	-0.105360516
1	0.8	-0.22314	0	-0.223143551
0	0.2	0	-0.22314	-0.223143551
0	0.1	0	-0.10536	-0.105360516
				$\Sigma =$ -0.657008134

The same calculations can be made for the second set of parameters.

Table 11. Example of calculation with *high*-probability values of bad

Y_i	P_i	$Y_i \times \ln P_i$	$(1-Y_i)\ln(1-P_i)$	$\{[Y_i \times \ln P_i] + [(1-Y_i)\ln(1-P_i)]\}$
				Log-likelihood function
1	0.1	-2.30259	0	-2.302585093
1	0.2	-1.60944	0	-1.609437912
0	0.8	0	-1.60944	-1.609437912
0	0.9	0	-2.30259	-2.302585093
				$\Sigma =$ -7.824046011

Again, the parameters that best produce the observed values show a higher value (i.e., lower negative values) to the *likelihood function*.

4.8 Parameters Estimation

The *maximum-likelihood*-parameters estimation tries to find parameters most likely to reproduce observed data. In practice, this means maximizing the log-likelihood function.

Hypothetically, one could construct a bivariate model according to the following steps:

1. Choose the parameters of the bivariate model, e.g., $\alpha = 1.5$ and $\beta = 0.6$;.
2. For the first case, multiply β by X and sum the product to the constant value α to obtain a prediction of the *logit* (if X is equal to 3 for the first case, the predicted *logit* is in accordance with [3]:

$$Z = logit$$
$$z = \alpha + \beta X$$
$$Z = 1.5 + 0.6 \times 3 = 3.3$$

3. Convert the *logit* into a probability using the formula [13]:

$$P_i = \frac{e^z}{1 + e^z}$$

For the first case, the probability is equal to:

$$P_i = \frac{e^{3.3}}{1 + e^{3.3}} = \frac{27.11264}{1 + 27.11264} = 0.9644$$

4. If $Y_i = 1$, then the contribution to the log-likelihood function for this case is in accordance with [22]:

$$\ln LF = \sum \{[Y_i \times \ln P_i] + [(1 - Y_i)\ln (1 - P_i)]\}$$

Note that, in this particular formulated hypothetical case ($\alpha = 1{,}5$ and $\beta = 0.6$), the sum (Σ) of the different variables (X_{ij}) is obviously not applicable.

$$\ln LF = 1 \times \ln 0.9644 + 0 \times \ln(1 - 0.9644) = -0.03622$$

Note that if there are more variables (X_{ij}): -, subscript "i" refers to the individual (e.g., John) and the subscript "j" refers to one of the different characteristics of John (e.g., marital status, age, etc.).

5. Repeat steps one to four for each of the other cases, and add up the components of the *log-likelihood function* to obtain the total value.

6. Repeat the steps up to another pair of parameters (α, β), and compare the *log-likelihood value* with the first set of parameters.

7. Proceed in this way for all the parameters, and choose those which have produced the highest *log-likelihood* value (i.e., the closest to 0).

The mathematical formulas and calculation procedures allow *logistic-regression* programs to more effectively identify the estimates that maximize the *log-likelihood function* (*LLF*).

Next, an algorithm is used to choose a new set of parameters in succession, producing larger *log likelihood* and better adjustments to the observed data. The process continues through repetitive cycles, or iterations, until the *maximization* of the *log-likelihood function* is achieved.

This process will be produced using statistical-package programs, such as SPSS, SAS, E-Views, and others.

Chapter 5

Tests of Significance Using Log-Likelihood Values

5.1 Difference between Probability and Likelihood

Probability and *likelihood* are two words that appear as synonyms in ordinary speech. However, statistically speaking, these words have different meanings.

Probability involves the relative possibility that an event will occur, and it is expressed by the ratio of the number of actual occurrences to the total number of possible occurrences. *Likelihood* serves as a reference or prediction, which does not involve the use of a strong base or a proven theory.

Likelihood refers to the possibility of events with different sets of parameter values, which may lead to a firm conclusion.

The *probability* of realization of an event is the ratio between the number of favorable cases to the realization of that event and the number of possible cases of that event, where f is the number of favorable cases and p the number of possible cases:

$$P_i = \frac{f}{p}$$

5.2 Likelihood Ratio Test

In large samples, the difference between the statistics of two log-likelihood models

$$[-2LLF_{0\ (initial\ or\ baseline\ model)} - (-2LLF_{1\ (final\ model\ or\ full\ model)})]$$

also called *likelihood ratio* (LR), reveals an approximation to the chi-square x^2.

The degrees of freedom (df) for the chi-square (x^2) test are equal to the difference in the number of parameters in the two models.

The LR statistic, as the F statistic in the multiple-linear regression, requires the identification of *two models* to be mutually compared, one of them being a special case of the other.

The largest model, which we shall denote by $LF_{1(final\ model)}$, is sometimes referred to as "full model," and the lowest, which we shall denote by $LF_{\emptyset(initial\ model)}$, is sometimes referred to as a "reduced model."

The *reduced model* is obtained equalizing β_{ij} parameters to 0 of the complete model. Thus, in the null hypothesis (H_0), to be tested, β_{ij} parameters of the complete model will be equal to 0.

The complete model that keeps the values of its coefficients represents the alternative hypothesis H_1:

$$\begin{cases} H_0: \beta_{i1}, \beta_{i2}, \ldots, \beta_{ij} = 0 \\ H_1: Exists\ at\ least\ one\ \beta_{ij} \neq 0 \end{cases}$$

The number of degrees of freedom (df) considered in the test of LR equals the number of parameters in the larger model.

To test the null hypothesis (H_0), the statistic used is LR, given by the equation:

$$LR = (-2) \times \ln\frac{LF_{\emptyset\ (initial\ model)}}{LF_{1\ (final\ model)}} \qquad [23]$$

Applying the property of logarithms:

$$\ln\frac{a}{b} = \ln a - \ln b$$

We obtain:

$$LR = (-2) \times (\ln LF_\emptyset - \ln LF_1)$$

$$LR =- 2\ln LF_\emptyset - (- 2\ln LF_1) \qquad [24]$$

5.3 Tests of Significance

The value of LLF reflects the likelihood of how data would be observed, given parameter estimates. It may be interpreted as a deviation from a saturated or perfect model in which log likelihood is equal to 0. The greater the value of log likelihood (i.e., negative value closest to 0), the better the parameters producing the observed data.

Although the LLF increases with efficiency parameters, its value has a somewhat less intuitive meaning because it depends on the sample size and the number of parameters, as well as the fit to the model. Accordingly, it requires a pattern to be compared with its relative dimension. One way to interpret *log-likelihood* dimension involves comparing the value of the final model (LLF_1) with the value of the initial model $(LLF_\emptyset)$ or the value of the base model, assuming all β_{ij} parameters are equal to 0.

The base value $(LLF_\emptyset)$ of the log likelihood, which comes from the insertion in the model of only the constant term α, is equivalent to using the average probability as the estimated value for all cases, i.e., 50 percent.

The greater the difference between the base value of log likelihood and log likelihood of the model, the better the model parameters (along the independent variables). This difference can be used in hypothesis testing (as well as in fitting or adjustment measures). As in the regression F test, the difference in the amount of the base model and the values of the log-likelihood model evaluates the null hypothesis (H_0), or $\beta_{i1} = \beta_{i2} = \ldots = \beta_{ik} = 0$. Not knowing X, the base model will use the average of (P_i) i.e., 50 percent—as predicted probability for each case, and under these conditions we will have:

Table 12. Example of calculation of LF_{Max} when $P_i = 0.5$

Y_i	P_i	$P_i^{Y_i}$	$(1-P_i)^{1-Y_i}$	$P_i^{Y_i} \times (1-P_i)^{1-Y_i}$ Likelihood function
1	0.5	0.5	1	0.5
1	0.5	0.5	1	0.5
0	0.5	1	0.5	0.5
0	0.5	1	0.5	0.5
				$LF_{Max} = \prod = 0.5 \times 0.5 \times 0.5 \times 0.5 = 0.0625$

Suppose that, with the knowledge of X, the full model will utilize values $P_i \neq 0.5$ (see table 13), and so the final model would be:

Table 13. Example of the calculation of LF_{Max} when $P_i \neq 0.5$

Y_i	P_i	$P_i^{Y_i}$	$(1-P_i)^{1-Y_i}$	$P_i^{Y_i} \times (1-P_i)^{1-Y_i}$ Likelihood function
1	0.9	0-9	1	0.9
1	0.8	0.8	1	0.8
0	0.2	1	0.8	0.8
0	0.1	1	0.9	0.9
				$LF_{Max} = \prod = 0.9 \times 0.8 \times 0.8 \times 0.9 = 0.5184$

Using values obtained for LF_{Max} (tables 12 and 13), we determine LLF_{Max}:

Table 14. Example of the calculation of likelihood ratio $-2(LLF)$

Model	Maximum-likelihood function (LF_{Max})	Log-likelihood function (LLF_{Max})	$-2(LLF)$ Likelihood ratio
Base model (LLF_0) (without explanatory	0.0625	-2.7726	5.5452

variables) (not knowing X)			
Final model (LLF_1) (with explanatory variables) (knowing X)	0.5184	- 0.6570	1.3140
Difference	- 0.4559	-2.1156	$x^2 = 4.2312$

If X is related to Y, knowing X (final model) should be close to 0, and it will reflect a better model than not knowing X (base model). Table 14 shows model improvement when it has knowledge of X.

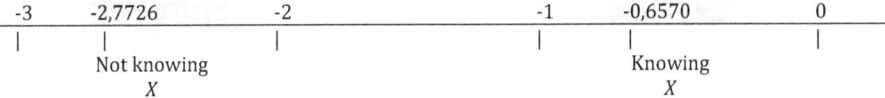

The significance test is made as follows:

1. Calculate the difference between base value LLF_0 and LLF_1 of the final model:

$$- 2.7726 - (- 0.6570) = - 2.1156.$$

2. Multiply that difference by -2, giving a value of chi-square (x^2) with a number of degrees of freedom equal to the number of independent variables, such as equal to the number of β parameters of the full model [not including constant (α)]:

$$- 2 \times (- 2.1156) = 4.2312.$$

3. The obtained value is compared with the values of the chi-square table for a given number of degrees of freedom (in our example $df = 1$).

The value of chi-square tests the null hypothesis H_0, which translates to all β coefficients being equal to 0.

When $\chi^2 = 0$, theoretical and observed probabilities agree exactly. In practice, expected probabilities are calculated based on a null hypothesis (H_0), such as when all the coefficients $\beta = 0$.

4. If the calculated value of χ^2 is greater than the tabulated value for a given level of significance, reject H_0.

Table 15. Decision against significance test

Calculated χ^2	4.2312
Tabulated $\chi^2_{0.95}$	3.841
Significance level	$\alpha = 0.05$
Degrees of freedom	1
Results	Calculated χ^2 > Tabulated $\chi^2_{0.95}$
Decision	Reject H_0, concluding that the independent variable significantly affects the dependent variable

Figure 4. Example of a χ^2 distribution for 1 df, showing the rejection against a certain critical value.

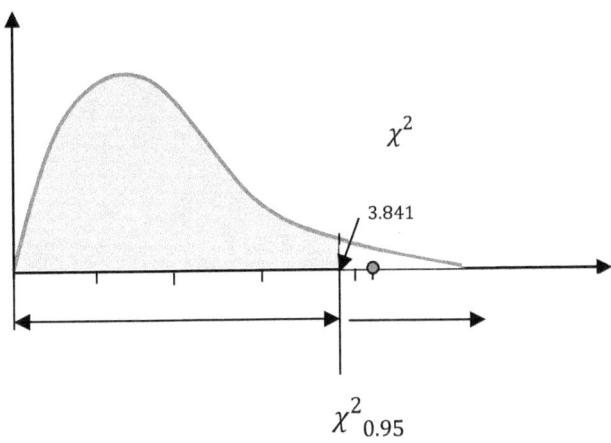

5. If calculated value of χ^2 is lower than the tabulated value, for a given level of significance, we accept H_0.

Table 16. Decision against significance test

Calculated χ^2	4.2312
Tabulated $\chi^2_{0.99}$	6.635
Significance level	$\alpha = 0.01$
Degrees of freedom	1
Results	Calculated χ^2 < Tabulated $\chi^2_{0.99}$
Decision	Accept H_0, concluding that independent variable does not significantly influence dependent variable

Figure 5. Example of a x^2 distribution for 1 df, showing the acceptance of H_0 against a certain critical value.

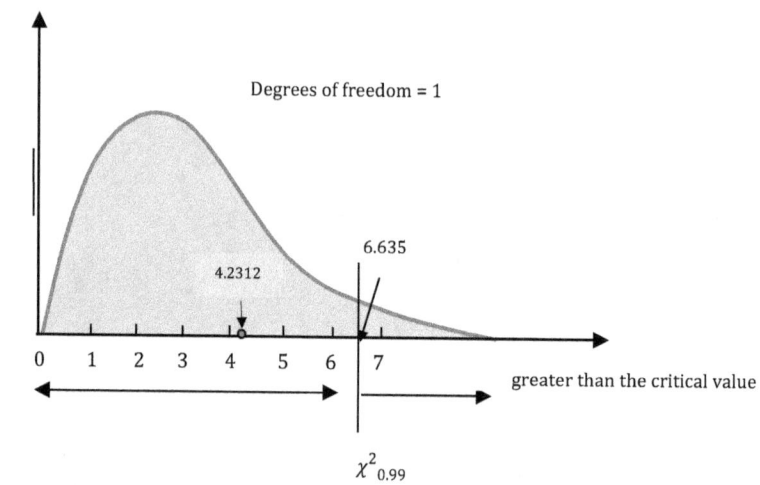

6. Check if the change in log-likelihood (LLF_{Max}) for all independent variables could have resulted in a change to the level of significance, i.e., whether the improvement in log likelihood is not significantly different from 0.

7. For a given degree of freedom, the greater the value of chi-square (x^2) the greater the model improvement compared to the base model and the less likely it is that all variable coefficients are equal to 0 in the population.

8. Multiply by -2 the result of the difference between the log-likelihood (LLF_{Max}) of the initial model and log-likelihood (LLF_{Max}) of the final model to obtain the value of chi-square:

$- 2 \times (- 2.1156) = 4.2312$

It will be equivalent to multiplying base model values and the initial model by -2, and then calculating the difference between them to measure improvement in the model:

$[-2 \times (-2.7726) - 2 \times (-0.6570)] = 4.2312$

In both situations, results are the same. However, we should keep in mind that, when multiplying by -2, the sign of log-likelihood values will be reversed.

The *maximum-likelihood* function of 0.5184 has a log-likelihood value of -0.6570 (table 14).

With a brief comparison of the baseline value (initial) and the final model value shown in table 14, we see some improvement by knowledge of X.

Although these figures have a small intuitive meaning, we can observe some improvement in the final model when compared with the base model.

With 1 degree of freedom for an independent variable, critical value of chi-square at $\alpha = 0.05$ $(\chi^2_{0.95})$ equals 3.8414.

Since current chi-square $\chi^2 = 4.2312$ at a significance level of $\alpha = 0.05$ $(\chi^2_{0.95})$ (is higher than critical value we shall conclude that the independent variable significantly affects dependent variable, i.e., it rejects H_0.

However, if the predetermined level of significance is $= 0.01$ $(\chi^2_{0.99})$, it is lower than the critical value 6.635 and then we shall conclude that the independent variable does not significantly influence the dependent variable—we accept H_0.

In this fictitious example, with only four cases, it becomes difficult to achieve any level of statistical significance, but it illustrates the use of the chi-square test.

In short, we can say that probability function values are between 0 and 1, while log-likelihood values range from $-\infty$ to 0.

The basic model shows that *likelihood function* and *log-likelihood function* values are lower than in the final model. The higher likelihood and log-likelihood values for final model in relation to base model values, the greater the improvement through the parameters other than 0.

Log-likelihood values times -2 whose amplitude varies from 0 to $+\infty$ reverse their meaning to be more in line with the common interpretation of error in regression models. The base model shows a higher value than the final model. The greater the differences between the two models, the greater the improvement observed in the model due to the independent variables.

Chi-square calculation can either be obtained from the difference of log-likelihoods between the initial and the final model $[-2.7726 - (-0.6570)] = -2.1156$, or from the logarithm of its ratio. The principle results from logarithm properties:

$$\ln a - \ln b = \ln \frac{a}{b}$$

In the given example, likelihood values ratio is $\frac{0.0625}{0.5184} = 0.12056327$, and the logarithm of that number is $\ln 0.12056327 = -2.1156$.

Multiplying the logarithm of the ratio by -2, we obtain the value of 4.2312, that is: $[-2.1156 \times (-2)] = 4.2312$.

Chapter 6

Evaluation of the Logistic Model

6.1 Introduction

The evaluation of the *logistic model* consists in verifying the quality of adherence of values produced by the model (estimated values) through their similarity with observed values.

This evaluation is done by various statistics, whose choice depends on the one that makes the best-fit estimation to the observed values.

Coefficient of determination (R^2) is one of those measures, but in the present study on *logistic regression*, it requires some preliminary considerations.

6.2 R^2 Statistic

Comparison between estimated and observed values is achieved through the total variance between those values and it is given by:

$$Total\ variance = \sum (Y_i - \bar{Y})^2 \qquad [25]$$

Where:
Y_i - observed values
$\bar{Y}$ - average value of observations

However, the statistical model cannot entirely explain the observed values, because errors and residuals, which are specific to an estimate, arise. We call this an *unexplained variance*, and it corresponds to the sum of squared difference between the observed value Y_i and the estimated value $\hat{Y}_i$ by the model for that observation.

$$Variance\ not\ explained = \sum (Y_i - \hat{Y}_i)^2 \qquad [26]$$

Where:

Y_i - observed values

$\hat{Y}_i$ - estimated values

The variance explained by the model is given by:

$$Variance\ explained = \sum (\hat{Y} - \overline{Y})^2 \qquad [27]$$

Where:

$\hat{Y}$ - estimated values

$\overline{Y}$ - average value of the observations

We conclude that the total variance is equal to the explained variance, plus the unexplained variance, namely:

Total variance = Variance explained + Variance not explained

From this equation, we can define the coefficient of determination R^2 as:

$$R^2 = \frac{Variance\ explained}{Total\ variance}$$

[28]

But:

$$Variance\ explained = Total\ variance - Variance\ not\ explained$$

And substituting in R^2:
$$R^2 = \frac{Total\ variance - Variance\ not\ explained}{Total\ variance}$$

Then:
$$R^2 = \frac{Total\ variance}{Total\ variance} - \frac{Variance\ not\ explained}{Total\ variance}$$

$$R^2 = 1 - \frac{Variance\ not\ explained}{Total\ variance}$$

Substituting by their values:

$$R^2 = 1 - \frac{\sum(Y_i - \hat{Y})^2}{\sum(Y_i - \bar{Y})^2}$$

[29]

Although the *dependent variable* in the *logistic regression* has no variance as continuous variables in linear regression, procedures of the *maximum-likelihood* function (LF_{Max}) provide adjustment to the model—similar to those measures used in regression by *least-squares method*. As in tests of significance, it makes sense to compare a statistical model in which we know the independent variables with another model in which we do not know them.

In simple *linear regression*, goodness of fit is achieved by the sum of squared deviations (errors, or residuals), as illustrated in figure 6.

Figure 6. Graphical representation of deviations in simple linear regression.

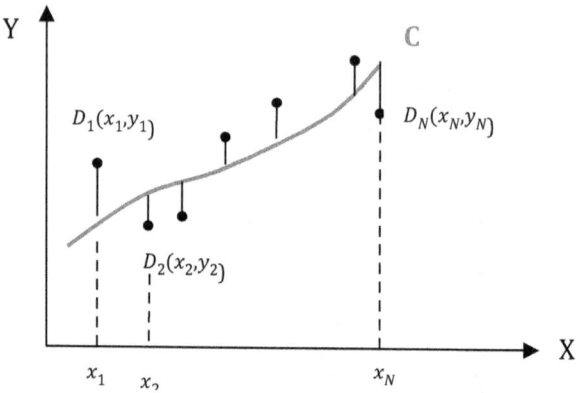

Of all the curves that fit a set of points, the one with the property to present minimum value of:

$$D_1^2 + D_2^2 + \ldots + D_N^2$$

is the one that best fits or adheres to the real situation and being called least-squares curve, and whose method is called *least-squares method*.

In this regression, the total sum of deviation squares $D_1^2 + D_2^2 + \ldots + D_N^2$ is a measure of the goodness of fit of the curve C (figure 6) to the presented data. If that sum is small, adjustment is good, otherwise the adjustment is bad.

The total sum of $D_1^2 + D_2^2 + \ldots + D_N^2$ can be split into two parcels called (1) *regression sum of squares* and (2) *error or residual sum of squares*.

A measure of the goodness of the least-squares line, as we said, is called coefficient of determination or R^2 given by:

$$R^2 = \frac{Regression\ sum\ of\ squares}{Total\ sum\ of\ squares}$$

but:

$$Regression\ sum\ of\ squares = Total\ sum\ of\ squares - Error\ sum\ of\ squares$$

where:

$$R^2 = \frac{Total\ sum\ of\ squares - Error\ sum\ of\ squares}{Total\ sum\ of\ squares}$$

$$R^2 = \frac{Total\ sum\ of\ squares}{Total\ sum\ of\ squares} - \frac{Error\ sum\ of\ squares}{Total\ sum\ of\ squares}$$

$$R^2 = 1 - \frac{Error\ sum\ of\ squares}{Total\ sum\ of\ squares}$$

Error sum of squares is the *variance not explained* by the least-squares line, and total sum of squares is the *total variance explained* by the least-squares line. Then R^2 is the proportion of *total sum of squares* explained by the least-squares line, and it must lie between 0 and 1, and it is reported as a percentage.

Let us take four pairs of coordinates (X,Y) to illustrate R^2 calculus.

Figure 7. Coordinate pairs (X, Y) to illustrate calculus.

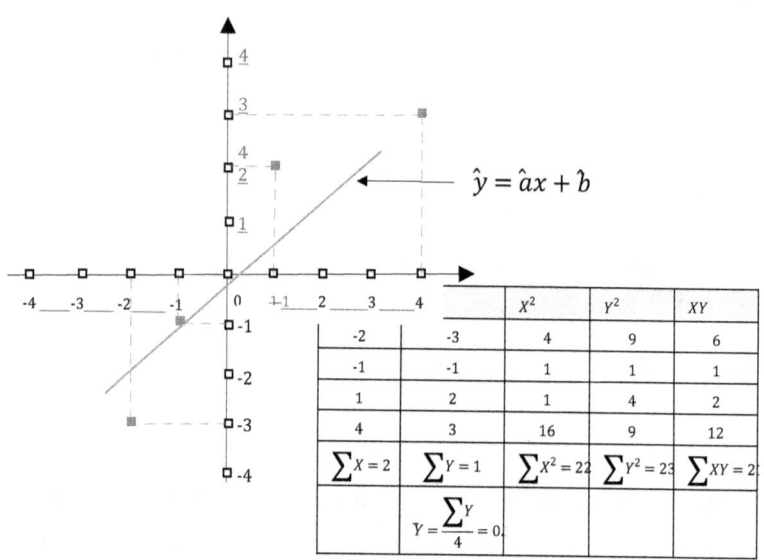

X	Y	X^2	Y^2	XY
-2	-3	4	9	6
-1	-1	1	1	1
1	2	1	4	2
4	3	16	9	12
$\sum X = 2$	$\sum Y = 1$	$\sum X^2 = 22$	$\sum Y^2 = 23$	$\sum XY = 21$
	$Y = \dfrac{\sum Y}{4} = 0.$			

$$\hat{y} = \hat{a}x + b$$

$$\hat{a} = \frac{(\sum X).(\sum Y) - n\sum XY}{(\sum X)^2 - n\sum X^2} = \frac{2 \times 1 - 4 \times 21}{4 - 4 \times 22} = \frac{-82}{-84} = 0.97619$$

$$b = \frac{(\sum X).(\sum XY) - (\sum Y)(\sum X^2)}{(\sum X)^2 - n\sum X^2} = \frac{2 \times 21 - 1 \times 22}{4 - 4 \times 22} = \frac{20}{-84} = -0.2381$$

$\hat{y}_1 = 0.97619(-2) - 0.2381 = -2.1$
$\hat{y}_2 = 0.97619(-1) - 0.2381 = -1.2$
$\hat{y}_3 = 0.97619(1) - 0.2381 = 0.738$
$\hat{y}_4 = 0.97619(4) - 0.2381 = 3.6666$

Total variance = $\sum (Y_i - \bar{Y})^2$
Total variance = $(-3 - 0.25)^2 + (-1 - 0.25)^2 + (2 - 0.25)^2 + (3 - 0.25)^2 = 22.750$
Variance NOT explained = $\sum (Y_i - \hat{Y}_i)^2$
Variance NOT explained = $(-3 + 2.19048)\text{\textasciicircum}2 + (-1 + 1.21429)\text{\textasciicircum}2 + (2 - 0.738095)\text{\textasciicircum}2 + (3$
Variance explained = $\sum (\hat{Y}_i - \bar{Y})^2$
Variance explained = $(-2.19048 - 0.25)^2 + (-1.21429 - 0.25)^2 + (0.738095 - 0.25)^2 + (3.$

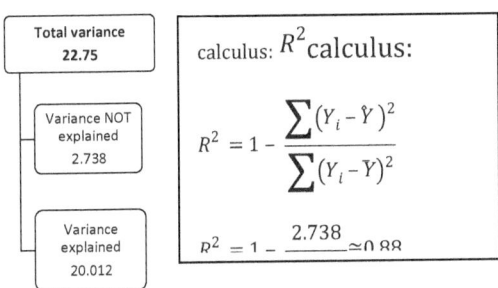

- Total variance 22.75
  - Variance NOT explained 2.738
  - Variance explained 20.012

calculus: R^2 calculus:

$$R^2 = 1 - \frac{\sum (Y_i - \hat{Y})^2}{\sum (Y_i - \bar{Y})^2}$$

$$R^2 = 1 - \frac{2.738}{} \approx 0.88$$

This example can be solved with SPSS, which displays the total sums of squares, error, and regression. SPSS command is: Analyze > Regression > Linear, producing the following output:

Variables entered/removed [a]

Model	Variables Entered	Variables removed	Method
1	x[b]		Enter

a. Dependent variable:y
b. All requested variables entered

Model summary

Model	R	R Square	Adjusted R Square	Std. Error of the Estimate
1	.938 [a]	.880	.819	1.17006

a. Predictors: Constant), x

ANOVA [a]

Model		Sum of Squares	df	Mean Square	F	Sig.
1	Regression	20.012	1	20.012	14.617	.062[b]
	Residual	2.738	2	1.369		
	Total	22.750	3			

a. Dependent variable: y
b. Predictors: (Constant), x

Coefficients [a]

Model	Unstandardized Coefficients	Standardized Coefficients	t	Sig.

		B	Std. Model	Beta		
1	(Constant)	-.238	.599		-.398	.729
	X	.976	.255	.938	3.823	.062

a. Dependent variable: y

6.3 R^2 Pseudo Statistic

As described above (see section 6.2), R^2 is a statistical measure that evaluates the adjustment quality of a regression linear model to the observed data in percentage terms. In the linear regression model, dependent variables are continuous, which is not the case of *logistic regression* where the dependent variable is dichotomous.

In *logistic regression*, the base model $(LLF_\emptyset) \times (-2)$ is the probability of producing the observed values weighted by the coefficients of the independent variables (β_{ij}) equal to 0 corresponding to the total sum of squares of the chi-square (x^2), whose expression is given by:

$$x^2 = \frac{(Y_1 - \hat{Y}_1)^2}{\hat{Y}_1} + \frac{(Y_2 - \hat{Y}_2)^2}{\hat{Y}_2} + ... + \frac{(Y_k - \hat{Y}_k)^2}{\hat{Y}_k}$$

[30]

where:

Y_i - observed values

$\hat{Y}_i$ - estimated values

The improved log-likelihood base model regarding log-likelihood model $(LLF_{1(final)})$, shows the improvement of adjustment for independent variables. Similarly, these two log-likelihood models

$(LLF_{\emptyset(initial)})$ and $(LLF_{1(final)})$ define a proportional reduction in regression error, given by coefficient of determination (R^2):

$$R^2 = \frac{[(-2 \times LFV_\emptyset) - (-2 \times LFV_1)]}{(-2 \times LFV_\emptyset)}$$

[31]

The numerator shows the reduction in model error due to independent variables, and the denominator shows the error without using the independent variables. The resulting value of this ratio R^2 shows the improvement in log likelihood in relation to the baseline model, and it will be 0 when all the β coefficients are equal to 0, with a maximum close to 1.

However, R^2 statistic is not the *explained variance* (deviations with a defined pattern) once LLF does not represent the sum of the deviation squares, $\sum (\hat{Y} - \bar{Y})^2$.

Therefore, this measure is not genuinely applicable, and it is known as a *pseudo* explained variance or pseudo R^2 *statistic*.

Another adjustment measure is based on the principle that log-likelihood value depends on the number of cases, i.e., the sample size N. Consequently, the value of the chi-square test for independent variables (or improvements in $(-2) \times$ log likelihood in the numerator of the equation [31]) can be taken as a proportion of the chi-squared plus the sample size [32]. Aldrich and Nelson (1984) presented the following measure for the explained *pseudo variance*:

$$R^2 = \frac{\chi^2}{(\chi^2 + N)}$$

[32]

Other measurements suggested by other authors—namely Zavoina and McKelvey (1975), Cox and Snell (1989), Nagelkerke (1991), Lon (1997), and so on—have been presented for the model evaluation.

In an article published in February 2013 by Paul Allison ("What Is the Best R-Squared for *Logistic Regression?*"), the question he raises is relevant: how can I tell if my model fits the data (observed)? According to the author of "Logistic Regression Using SAS," there are two approaches to answer this question. One is to measure how well one can predict the dependent variable based on the independent variables.

The other one is to test whether the model needs to be specifically more complex or whether the model requires additional nonlinearities and interactions to satisfactorily represent observed data. Allison, in the cited article, says that, unfortunately, there are many different ways to calculate R^2 for *logistic regression,* and there has not yet been consensus on the matter. Some examples include Mittlbock and Schemper (1996), who present twelve different ways, and Menard (2000) considers seven different ones. The two most frequently reported methods in statistical software are proposed by McFadden (1974) and Cox and Snell (1989).

6.3.1 McFadden's R^2

Logistic regression is obviously estimated by *maximum-likelihood* function (LF_{Max}).

Being LF_0 the value of the likelihood function for a model with no predictors (independent variables), i.e., the initial base model, where all coefficients $\beta = 0$.

Being LF_1 the value of the *maximum-likelihood* function for the estimated model, or also referred to herein as the final model, McFadden defined R^2 as:

$$R^2 = 1 - \frac{\ln(LF_1)}{\ln(LF_\emptyset)}$$

[33]

The rationale of this formula is that $\ln(LF_\emptyset)$ has an analogous role to the squares residual value (variance not explained) in the linear regression. Consequently, this formula corresponds to a proportional reduction in the error variance. It is sometimes referred to as pseudo R^2.

6.3.2 Cox and Snell's R^2

These authors define as:

$$R^2 = 1 - \left(\frac{LF_\emptyset}{LF_1}\right)^{\frac{2}{n}}$$

[34]

Where N is the sample size. The rationale of this formula is that, for traditional linear regression theory, it means generality, or in other words, the usual R^2 for the linear regression since it depends on the assumed probability by models with and without predictors. Contrary to McFadden's R^2, applying the method of least squares as a special case.

According to Allison (2013), Cox and Snell's R^2 is much more attractive, especially since the formula can naturally be extended to other species estimated by *maximum-likelihood* regression, as in the case of negative binomial regression for counting data or Weibull survival time.

Table 17. Different statistics for evaluating *logistic model*

	Model Summary		
Step	-2 Log likelihood	Cox & Snell R Square	Nagelkerke R Square

1	2550.238[a]	.445	.594
2	1534.729[b]	.596	.795
3	1530.688[b]	.597	.796
4	1525.792[b]	.597	.796
5	1509.449[b]	.599	.799
a. Estimation terminated at iteration number 5 because parameter estimates changed by less than .001.			
b. Estimation terminated at iteration number 8 because parameter estimates changed by less than .001.			

6.4 Statistical Software Packages for Logistic Regression

Software programs for *logistic regression* predict the dichotomous-dependent variable group based on a typical cutoff value of 0.5, where cases with predicted probabilities higher than 0.5 are classified in dependent variable by 1, and those cases with predicted probabilities of 0.5 or below are classified as 0.

A short summary of the model efficiency is given by the percentage success rate obtained in all cases, or in correct classification, revealed by the dependent variable. In the course of this study, we present excerpts of the case study exemplifying some of these references and shown in chapter 8.

6.5 Z-Wald Test

The Wald test is also used in *logistic regression* to determine the significance of *logistic-regression* coefficients. Its interpretation is similar to the one done to $"F"$ values (in Fisher/Snedecor distribution) or $"t"$ (Student distribution) and used to test the significance of regression coefficients.

In multiple regression, $"t"$ value is used to access the significance of each coefficient. *Logistic regression* uses a different statistic, the Wald statistic. This enables the value of the statistical significance for each estimated coefficient to be made in such a way that hypothesis testing may occur precisely, as in the multiple regression.

If the logistic coefficients are statistically significant, we can interpret them in terms of their impact on the estimated probability and, thus, in the prediction of the individual in his/her group, i.e., the group granted credit (1) or the other group that has been refused credit (0).

The *Z-Wald* test is usually done when there is only one parameter to be tested, for example, when comparing the $LFV_\emptyset$ (initial) model with LFV_1 (final) model.

The *Z-Wald* test statistic is calculated by dividing the estimated coefficient by its standard error. This statistical *Z test*, with $z = \dfrac{\hat{\beta}}{s_{\hat{\beta}}}$, has approximately a normal distribution (0.1) [meaning average 0 and variance 1] in large samples. The square of statistic is approximately chi-square statistic with 1 degree of freedom. This is why the Wald statistic is so easy to calculate: divide the coefficient by the estimated standard error and then square the result.

When doing the Wald test, the required information is usually available in the output of the statistical package being used, which lists each model variable, followed by its *maximum-likelihood* coefficient and its standard error, as illustrated in table 18.

Table 18. Independent variables X_k and their *maximum-likelihood* coefficients, standard deviation, and chi-square

Independent variable	Coefficient of *maximum likelihood*	Standard deviation	Chi-square	p-value
X_1	β_1	s_{β_1}	χ^2	p
X_2	β_2	s_{β_2}	χ^2	p
...	...	...	χ^2	p
X_j	β_j	s_{β_j}	χ^2	p
...	...	...	χ^2	p
X_k	β_k	s_{β_k}	χ^2	p

Some statistical packages also calculate chi-square statistic and *p-value*. When examining the output, the user must find the corresponding line to the variable under analysis and calculate the *maximum-likelihood* coefficient ratio, β by its standard error s_{β_j} or read the chi-square statistic and its corresponding *p-value*.

The statistics of the log-likelihood ratio and its corresponding squared Wald statistics give approximately the same value in very large samples. Thus, if the sample is sufficiently large, the statistics used do not matter. Nevertheless, in moderate or small samples, the two statistics can give very different results. Statisticians, such as Hauk and Donner (1977) and Jennings (1986), have shown that log-likelihood statistical ratio is better than Wald statistics in such situations. Thus, when in doubt, it is recommended to use the statistical log-likelihood ratio.

Table 19. Output example of a statistical package illustrating Wald-test result

	Coefficient	S.E. Standard Error	Wald	df Degrees of Freedom	Sig. Significance	Exp (e^β)
gender	0.484417312	0.191595161	6.392492698	1	0.01	1.623228898
scoring	0.072706977	0.004523686	258.3255432	1	0.00	1.075415369
credit_lim it	0.000243156	1.94985E-05	155.5132213	1	0.00	1.000243186
current_ balance	0.000400667	0.0001147	12.20229734	1	0.00	1.000400747
revolving	-0.000472119	0.000122764	14.78971818	1	0.00	0.999527992
Constant	-53.97826127	3.268262466	272.7746012	1	0.00	3.61026E-24

From a statistical package output, we have drawn, by way of example, table 19, illustrating a Wald-test result as being the squared ratio between the independent variable estimation coefficient (β) and its standard error (s_β) :

$$Wald = \left(\frac{\beta}{s_\beta}\right)^2 \qquad [35]$$

Example: independent variable gender

$$Wald = \left(\frac{0.484417312}{0.191595161}\right)^2 = (2.528337926)^2 = 6.392492698$$

Chapter 7

ROC Curves

7.1 Introduction

This chapter describes and illustrates a graphical method that allows us to understand adjustment in cases where the *logistic model* predicted 0 or 1 classification, as reported in the presence of explanatory variables.

However, the prediction model will not hit 100 percent of the cases, and there are situations labeled with 0 even though it should have them rated 1, and vice versa, after having observed that some credit candidate showed a different behavior from the one predicted by the model.

The ROC acronym means *Receiver Operating Characteristics,* and it was developed during World War II (1939–1945 to identify objects as a real danger and distinguish them by their characteristics from those signals that were simple noises by Radar (*Radio Detection and Ranging*), an electromagnetic signal for covering long distances.

This concept has been applied in various science fields, particularly in medicine, radiology, prospecting data (data mining), credit scoring, and others.

7.2 Signal-Detection Theory

As mentioned in section 7.1, detection of electromagnetic signals in the presence of noise, which supported the signal-characteristics receiver model, was initially studied as a problem of statistical hypothesis. *Noise* (identified here as *bad* payer) was associated with the null hypothesis, H_0, while *noise* plus *signal* (identified here as *good* payer) was associated with the alternative hypothesis, H_1.

In radar identification context, *type I errors* were called *false alarms* and have their correspondence in credit scoring by *false positives*, i.e., bad payers who were classified as good payers. In the same radar-detection context, *type II errors* were designated as *failures* whose correspondence in credit scoring means *false negatives*, i.e., good payers who were classified as bad payers. In both situations, there is a danger, either by extending credit to a bad debtor or refusing credit to a good payer, because both situations involve very high costs.

In signal-detection theory, the observer (risk manager) has the responsibility to decide on the basis of randomness (based on his/her credit-analyst experience) whose stimulus is *signal + noise* (if the customer in question is a good payer) or *noise* (if the customer in question is defaulting).

The risk manager/credit analyst, after evaluating the credit application, must decide yes or no, or 1 or 0.

Designated by $P(good)$, the probability associated with the presence of *noise+signal,* and $P(bad)$, the probability associated only to *noise*, the sum of the two probabilities is equal to the unit:

$P(Good) + P(Bad) = 1$

For example, the probability of a customer being 70 percent good also means the probability of being 30 percent bad.

Credit-analyst decisions lie in a very narrow score range, and he/she may take a decision supported by a probability decision tree, which explains his/her decision regarding the credit request. Representing the decision tree that describes risk-manager behavior regarding a credit demand and agreeing with numbers significance, we have:

Table 20. The four credit-analyst decisions

1	Correctly accepted
2	Incorrectly refused

| 3 | Correctly refused |
| 4 | Incorrectly accepted |

Figure 8. The four credit-manager decisions.

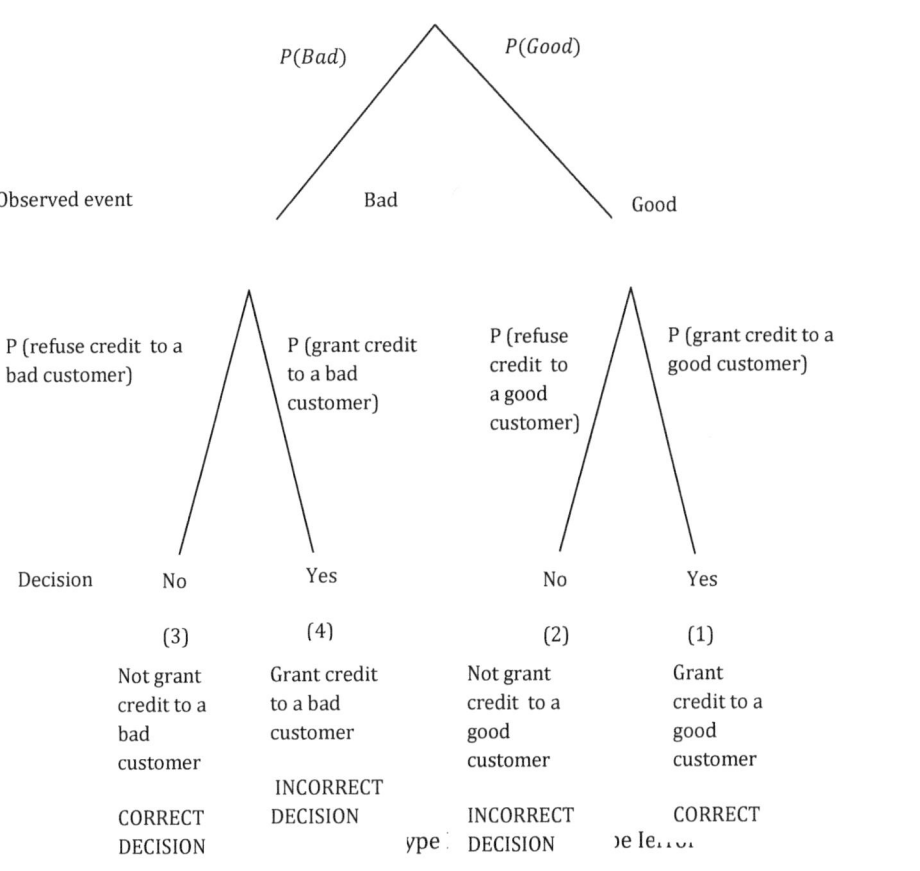

7.2.1 Signal Detection

In signal detection, we built a graph that illustrates the performance of a binary (0 or 1) classification system, and we have differentiated true signs (actually true) from true signals (but which, after all, were false alarms). The first ones have been conventionally designated by *true positives* (TP) and the latter by *false positive* (FP), or *type I errors*.

The same principle was applied to differentiate between the sounds (TN) from those which were not hoaxes but *failures*, known as *false negative* (FN), or *type II errors*.

With these four categories $(TP, FP, FN, and\ TN)$, it was possible to establish percentages, or rates of error and accuracy, depending on the produced results.

In geometric terms, the ROC curve is a graphic representation of coordinates wherein the abscissae is registered *(1-specificity)*, and in the ordinates it is *sensitivity*. The coordinate values represent probability measurements, thus, they vary between 0 and 1.

Sensitivity and *specificity* are used to determine accuracy or error percentages in relation to what the model has predicted and what was observed on a point of separation between good and bad payers, which is called *cutoff*.

Thus the *error rate* is obtained by the following ratio:

$$Error\ Rate = \frac{FN + FP}{TP + FN + FP + TN}$$

[36]

And the *hit rate:*

$$Hit\ rate = \frac{TN + TP}{TP + FN + FP + TN}$$

[37]

The same value is obtained by:

$Hit\ rate = 1 - Error\ rate$

$Hit\ rate = 1 - \dfrac{FN + FP}{TP + FN + FP + TN}$

$$Hit\ rate = \frac{TP + FN + FP + TN - FN - FP}{TP + FN + FP + TN}$$

$$Hit\ rate = \frac{TN + TP}{TP + FN + FP + TN}$$

The most common way to report the accuracy of a binary forecast is by using separately true positives (or false positives) and true negatives (or false negatives). In other words, separating the positive signs from the negative ones, whether true or false.

Thus, four other measures are identified, which serve to calibrate the predictive system:

$$Sensitivity = True\ Positive\ Rate = \frac{TP}{TP + FN} \quad [38]$$

$$False\ Positive\ Rate = \frac{FP}{FP + TN} \quad [39]$$

$$Specificity = True\ Negative\ Rate = \frac{TN}{TN + FP} \quad [40]$$

$$False\ Negative\ Rate = \frac{FN}{TP + FN} \quad [41]$$

True positive rate (TPR) is also known as *sensitivity* and *true negative rate* (TNR) as *specificity*.

$TPR + FNR = 1$

We can also define similar measurements using positive values $(TP + FP)$ and negative values $(TN + FN)$ as a denominator, taking the designations of positive predictive value (PPV) and negative predictive value, (NPV) as following :

$$Sensitivity = Positive\ Predictive\ Value = \frac{TP}{TP + FP} \quad [42]$$

$$Specificity = Negative\ Predictive\ Value = \frac{TN}{TN + FN} \quad [43]$$

In this criteria, positive predictive value is called *sensitivity*, and negative predictive value is *specificity*.

7.3 Statistical Theory

In terms of making statistical decisions, the distribution of bad payers (left-side distribution) represents null hypothesis, (H_0), and the distribution of good payers (right-side distribution) represents alternative hypothesis, (H_1).

Thus, the hypothesis of the credit-granting issue may be specified as:

H_0: Bad payer population has *mean (average)* : $\mu = \mu_0$

H_1: Good payer population has *mean (average)*: $\mu = \mu_1$

Based on observation, one of the hypotheses is accepted.

Distribution of good and bad payers, cutoff score, and their means (averages):

Figure 9. Distribution of good and bad payers, cutoff score, and their means (averages).

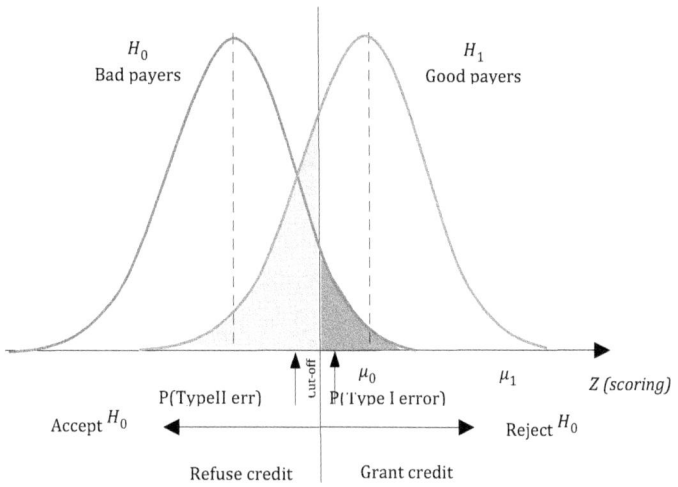

Table 21. Acceptance and rejection of H_0

		Observed	
		H_0 Bad payers	H_1 Good payers
Test Result	Accept H_0 - Accept Bad payers	OK	Type II Error
	Reject H_0 (Accept H_1 - Accept Good payers)	Type I Error	OK

The right, shaded area, cutoff side represents the probability of making a type I error, which corresponds to the probability of granting credit to a bad payer, i.e., rejecting H_0 when H_0 is true.

The left side, cutoff, shaded area represents the probability of committing a type II error, which corresponds to the probability of refusing credit to a good payer, i.e., accepting H_0 when H_1 is true.

Consider a frontier point (scoring) on the abscissa, known as *cutoff*. According to this criterion placement, all customers above that point will be classified as good payers and customers below that point will be classified as bad payers. That is, the construction of the statistical test is equivalent to dividing the abscissa axe (scorings) into two zones separated by the *cutoff*.

Thus, scorings below the cutoff will lead to acceptance of null hypothesis H_0, and above the cutoff scorings leads to acceptance of alternative hypothesis H_1. Depending on the chosen criterion for the cutoff positioning, it will be possible to determine the probability of committing a type I or type II error.

The most common statistical rule is to establish the probability of committing a type I error arbitrarily at a significance level of 0.05 or 0.01 and then choosing a criterion that lessens the likelihood of committing a type II error.

Neyman and Pearson (1933) demonstrated that the best test is defined in terms of *likelihood ratio*. We accept when the *likelihood ratio* exceeds a certain cutoff value chosen to produce the desired probability of committing a type I error.

The power test is defined by:

$$k = \begin{cases} Probability\ (commiting\ Type\ I\ error) & under\ H_0 \\ 1 - Probability\ (commiting\ Type\ II\ error) & under\ H_1 \end{cases}$$

According to Neyman and Pearson (1933), we set up the probability of committing a type I error and pick up the *likelihood ratio* equal to the cutoff to maximize the power of the test. Thus, we may draw the operating characteristic curves:

Figure 10. *Sensitivity* and *specificity* versus scoring.

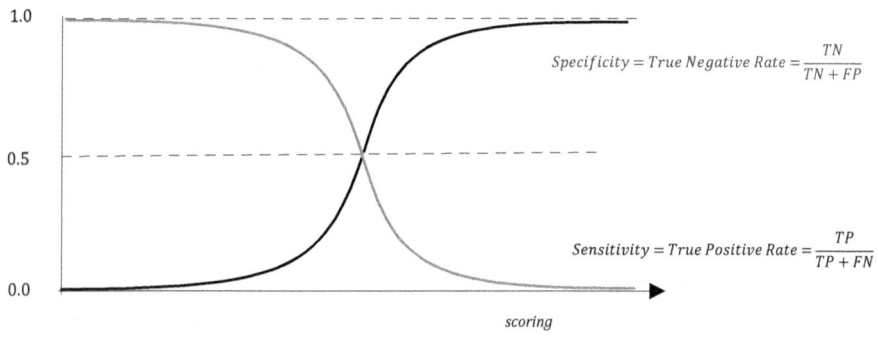

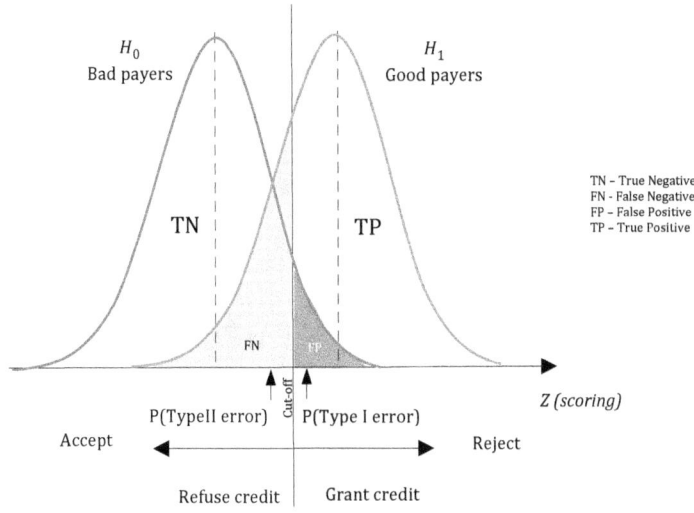

Figure 11. Type I errors (false positive) and type II errors (false negative).

Figures 12–13. False-positive rate (1-TNR—shaded area) decreases when cutoff score is higher. This increases *specificity* (TNR), but *sensivity* (TPR) will be reduced.

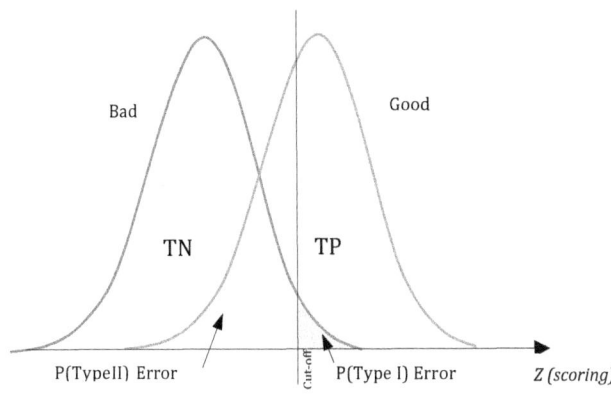

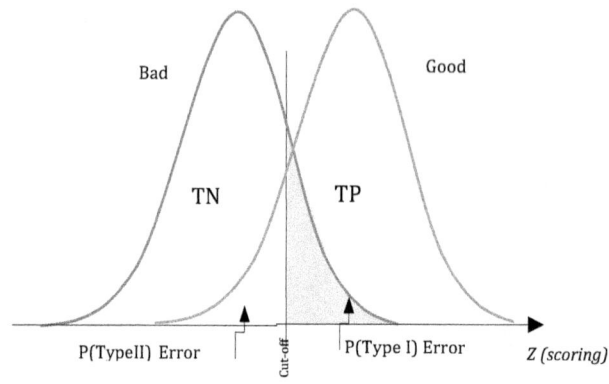

When choosing a high scoring value (cutoff) as the separation point, $False\ Positive\ Rate = \dfrac{FP}{FP+TN}$ decreases, increasing *specificity* (*TNR*), but otherwise $True\ Positive\ Rate = \dfrac{TP}{TP+FN}$ (*sensitivity*) will be reduced.

7.4 Confusion Matrix

For viewing the abovementioned measurements, we now present a matrix that will illustrate its usefulness in determining those values referred to in section 7.1 and its contribution to the development of the ROC curve.

Suppose you know, a priori, the classification given by a financial institution specializing in consumer credit, which chose 1,600 of its customers who showed a compliant profile (with reduced credit risk, i.e., classified with 1) and another 1,600 who, in the course of their business relationship with the financial institution, failed to comply with their commitments and, therefore, they were unfavorably classified (with high credit risk, i.e, classified 0).

Subsequently, the 3,200 customers were randomly collected in a database to which the *logistic model* has been applied to evaluate the model accuracy. If the model was 100 percent infallible, it would classify 1,600 customers as good (1) and 1,600 as potentially bad (0).

However, these models are not infallible, and they may predict a rating not in accordance with the observed result. The output presented by the *logistic model* was the following:

From 1,600 customers currently defaulting (bad), the model ranked 1,433 as defaulting (bad) and 126 as compliant (good).

From 1,600 customers currently compliant (good), the model ranked 1,474 as compliant (good) and 167 as defaulting (bad).

Thus, from the 3,200 customers, the *logistic model* correctly ranked (1,474 + 1,433 = 2,907 customers) and failed (126 + 167 = 293).

Through these results, it is possible to construct a confusion matrix:

Table 22. Confusion matrix

		Expected	
		Good	Bad
Observed	Good	True positive	False negative (type II error)
	Bad	False positive (type I error)	True negative

Table 23. Confusion matrix illustrating values obtained in the case study (chapter 8)

		Classification estimated by *logistic model*	
		Good ("1")	Bad ("0")
Current observed classification	Good("1")	TP = 1474	FN = 167
	Bad ("0")	FP = 126	TN = 1433
	Total	TP+FP=1600	FN+TN=1600

Interpreting the confusion matrix, we could, therefore, determine the hit rate and the error rate of the predictive model.

$$Hit\ rate = \frac{TN + TP}{TP + FN + FP + TN} = \frac{1433 + 1474}{1474 + 167 + 126 + 1433} = \frac{2907}{3200} = 0.9084 = 90.84\%$$

$$Error\ rate = \frac{FN + FP}{TP + FN + FP + TN} = \frac{167 + 126}{1474 + 167 + 126 + 1433} = \frac{293}{3200} = 0.0916 = 9.16\%$$

Continuing with the calculation of different rates that can be removed from the confusion matrix, we obtain:

$$True\ Posive\ Rate = \frac{TP}{TP + FN} = \frac{1474}{1474 + 167} = \frac{1474}{1641} = 0.8982 = 89.82\%$$

$$False\ Negative\ Rate = \frac{FN}{TP + FN} = \frac{167}{1474 + 167} = \frac{167}{1641} = 0.1018 = 10.18\%$$

$TPR + FNR = 100\%$

$$True\ Negative\ Rate = \frac{TN}{TN + FP} = \frac{1433}{1433 + 126} = \frac{1433}{1559} = 0.9192 = 91.92\%$$

$$False\ Positive\ Rate = \frac{FP}{TN + FP} = \frac{126}{1433 + 126} = \frac{126}{1559} = 0.0808 = 8.08\%$$

$TNR + FPR = 100$

The following summary table shows the different values for *sensitivity* and *specificity* in relation to each of the adopted criteria:

Table 24. Adopted criteria for determining *sensitivity* and *specificity* values

Sensitivity	Specificity
$TPR = \frac{TP}{TP + FN} = \frac{1474}{1474 + 167} = \frac{1474}{1641} = 89.8$	$TNR = \frac{TN}{TN + FP} = \frac{1433}{1433 + 126} = \frac{1433}{1559} = 91,$
$PPV = \frac{TP}{TP + FP} = \frac{1474}{1474 + 126} = \frac{1474}{1600} = 92.1$	$NPV = \frac{TN}{TN + FN} = \frac{1433}{1433 + 167} = \frac{1433}{1600} = 89.$

Positive predictive value error (*sensitivity*) is as follows:

$PPV\ error = 1 - PPV$

$PPV\ error = 1 - 0.9213 = 0.0787 = 7.87\%$

Negative predictive value error (*specificity*) will be:

$NPV\ error = 1 - NPV$

$NPV\ error = 1 - 0.8956 = 0.1044 = 10.44\%$

7.5 Computer-Program Outputs

Each computer-software manufacturer opts for different criteria for presentation of measures for building the ROC curve coordinates, i.e., the *sensitivity* in the ordinates, and *1-specificity* in the abscissae.

We present an output of E-Views obtained through a sample of 3,200 credit-card users of a financial institution and relating it with the confusion matrix for the same practical example we have been using.

Table 25. Output of E-Views illustrating the results obtained in the case study
(chapter 8)

Expectation-Prediction Evaluation for Binary Specification
Success cutoff: C=0.5

	Estimated Equation			Constant Probability		
	Dep= 0	Dep= 1	Total	Dep= 0	Dep= 1	Total
P(Dep= 1)<=C	1433	126	1559	1600	1600	3200
P(Dep=1)>C	167	1474	1641	0	0	0
Total	1600	1600	3200	1600	1600	3200
Correct	1433	1474	2907	1600	0	1600
% Correct	89.56	92.13	90.84	100.00	0.00	50.00
% Incorrect	10.44	7.87	9.16	0.00	100.00	50.00
Total Gain	-10,44	92.13	40.84			
Percent Gain	NA	92.13	81.69			

	Estimated Equation			Constant Probability		
	Dep= 0	Dep= 1	Total	Dep= 0	Dep= 1	Total
E(#of Dep= 0)	1374.32	226.03	1600.36	800.00	800.00	1600.00
E(#of Dep= 1)	225.68	1373.97	1599.64	800.00	800.00	1600.00
Total	1600.00	1600.00	3200.00	1600.00	1600.00	3200.00
Correct	1374.32	1373.97	2748.29	800.00	800.00	1600.00
% Correct	85.90	85.87	85.88	50.00	50.00	50.00
% Incorrect	14.10	14.13	14.12	50.00	50.00	50.00
Total Gain*	35.90	35.87	35.88			
Percent Gain	71.79	71.75	71.77			

*Change in" % Correct" from default (constant probability) specification

**Percent of incorrect (default) prediction corrected by equation

Table 26. SPSS output—confusion matrix illustrating the *in-sample* results (chapter 8)

		Estimated classification by logistic model	
		Good ("1")	Bad ("0")
Current classification (Observed)	Good ("1")	TP= 1474	FN=167
	Bad ("0")	FP= 126	TN=1433
	Total	TP+FP= 1600	FN+TN=1600

Through the presented calculations, we can visualize the matching values and their meaning and interpretation with the E-Views output values.

The same analysis can be obtained through SPSS:

Table 27. SPSS output—confusion matrix illustrating the results of the case study (chapter 8)

Classification Table [a]					
	Observed		Predicted		
			COD		Percentage correct
			0	1	
Step 1	COD	0	1409	191	88.1
		1	327	1272	79.5
	Overall percentage				83.8
Step 2	COD	0	1433	126	89.6
		1	167	1474	92.1
	Overall percentage				90.8
a. The cut value is, 500					

And through SAS:

Table 28. SAS output illustrating the results of the case study (chapter 8)

		Observed		
		Good	Bad	Total
Predicted	Good	TP=1 474 46.06% PPV=92,13% Sensiv.=89.82%	FP=126 3.94% 7.88% 8.08%	1 600 50.00%
	Bad	FN=167 5,22% 10.44% 10.18%	TN=1 433 44.78% NPV=89.56% Specif.=91.92%	1 600 50.00%
	Total	1 641 51.28%	1 559 48.72%	3 200 100.00%

Each one of these cells contains very useful information. For example, the error rate is given by the sum of 3.94%+5.22% = 9.16%.

PPV and NPV can be found between the lines of percentages. Here PPV is 92.13 percent, and NPV is 89.56 percent. Finally, *sensitivity* (TPR) and *specificity* (TNR) are available in the column of percentages, and they are equal, respectively, to 89.82 percent and 91.92 percent.

7.6 ROC Curves Graphic Layout

It is very important to understand the correct interpretation of *sensitivity*, *specificity*, PPV, and NPV. Let us start with the *predicted* values. Their denominators are the values of the *predictions* of good and bad customers (1,600 good and 1,600 bad). PPV values can be interpreted as the probability of hitting a current good customer when predicting his/her ranking as good, and NPV is the probability of observing a bad client when the prediction is bad.

Once a good customer is predictable, the probability of observing as being good is estimated at 92.13 percent. Similarly, if the prediction is bad, then the probability of being bad today is estimated at 89.56 percent.

In contrast, the denominators for *sensitivity* and *specificity* are the observed values as positive and negative. Therefore, *sensitivity* is the probability that a good customer is correctly identified by the prediction; similarly, *specificity* is the probability that a bad customer is correctly identified by the prediction. In our example, the probability that a bood customer is correctly predicted is 89.82 percent, and the probability that a bad customer is correctly predicted is 91.92 percent. Now we consider the problem that naturally leads to using the ROC curve. Suppose we want to predict a binary outcome, such as good and bad, but instead of having an explanatory binary variable, we have a continuous variable. Once we know how to analyze the predictive accuracy for a binary predictor (using percentages such as *sensitivity* and *specificity*), we should consider the transformation of the predicted probability into a dichotomous probability using a certain level (for example, a given score or score range for the cutoff).

The results, however, are clearly dependent on the choice of that level (cutoff). The question is how can we use the various levels and report the results for each one of them?

The ROC curve offers a way to solve this question, focusing simply on *sensitivity* and *1- specificity*. For a better understanding, we must analyze table 29.

Figure 14 is a histogram of customers distributed by score ranges of good and bad payers. A very high score—higher than 726—almost implies the existence of a good payer. In the score range of 726 to 730, 92 percent are good payers; in the range 731 to 735, 88 percent are good payers; in the range 741 to 745, 90 percent are good payers; in the range 746 the 750, 95 percent are good payers.

Table 29. Different score ranges used in the construction of the ROC curve

Score	691-695	696-700	701-705	706-710	711-715	716-720	721-725	726-730	731-735	736-740	741-745	746-750	751-755	756-760	765-770
Good	21	82	20	93	62	401	47	708	128	218	113	56	3	22	0
Bad	130	115	68	79	81	64	34	63	17	23	12	3	0	2	0

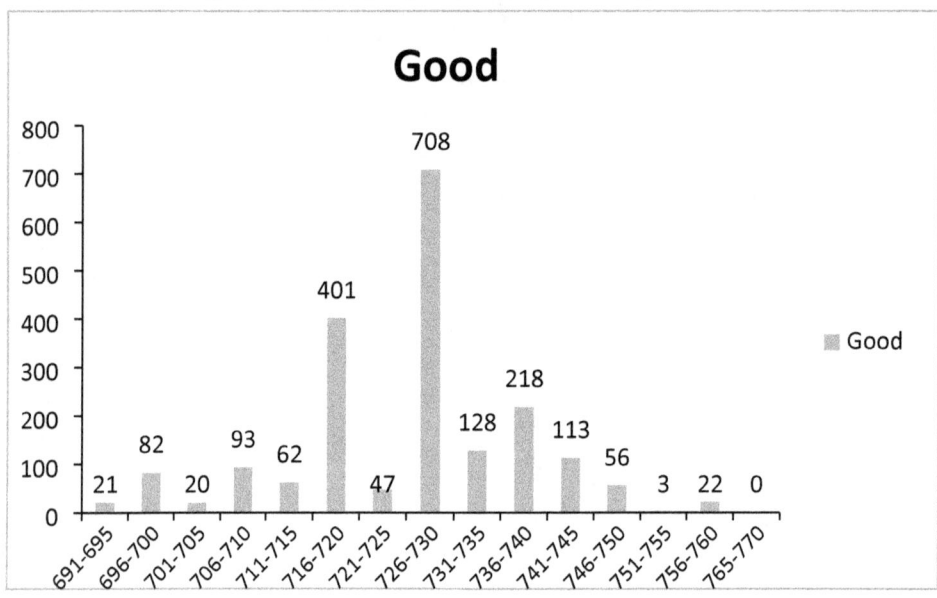

Figure 14. Frequency of good and bad by score ranges.

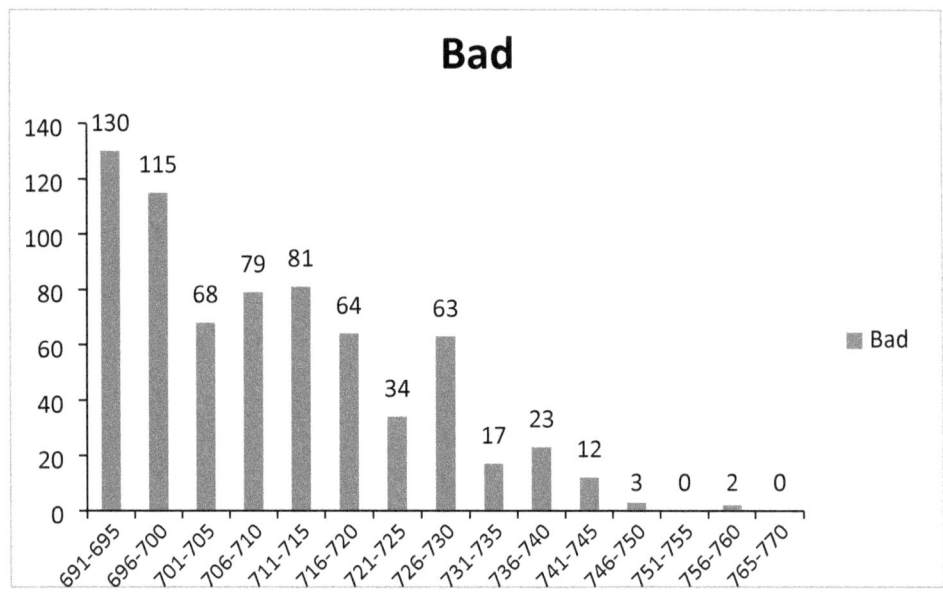

The biggest doubts lie in the smaller ranges, showing some overlap between the distributions of good and bad in a gray zone: 696 to 700, 701 to 705, 710 to 706, and 711 to 715, in which the percentage of good is 42, 23, 54, and 43 percent, respectively. How to position the cutoff most correctly? One way is to calculate *sensitivity* and *specificity* for various cutoffs in that gray area.

The given example has considered four ranges for cutoff placement: 696 to 700, 701 to 705, 706 to 710, and 711 to 715.

Figure 15. Good and bad distributions by score.

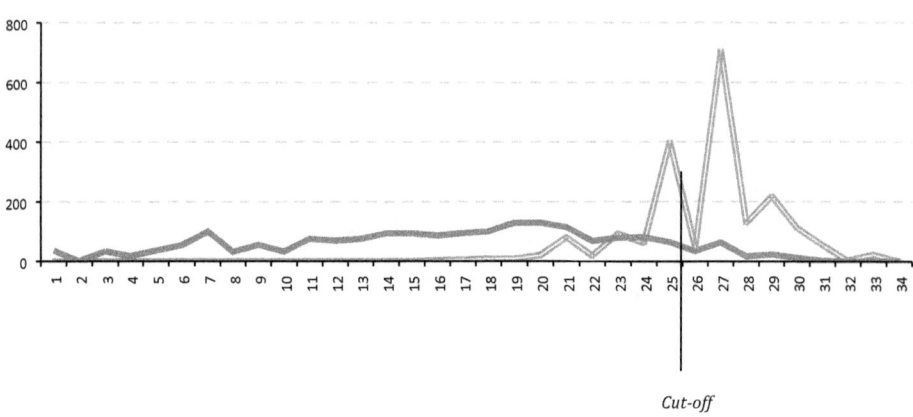

Previous analysis can be repeated for multiple ranges of cut-off scores, each one producing different values for *sensitivity* and *specificity*. The values for these indicators will be obtained through a confusion matrix for each selected cut-off.

The graph obtained through SPSS interprets sensitivity and specificity values, for each variable individually or for all, as shown below.

Table 30. Calculation of *sensivity* and *specificity* values for different score ranges

	A 696-700 Standard reference			B 701-705 Standard reference			C 706-710 Standard reference			D 711-715 Standard reference		
	Good	Bad	Tot	Good	Bad	Tot	Good	Bad	Tot	Good	Bad	Tot
Good	TP 72	FN 14	86	TP 15	FN 5	20	TP 83	FN 7	90	TP 56	FN 8	64
Bad	FP 10	TN 101	111	FP 5	TN 63	68	FP 10	TN 72	82	FP 6	TN 73	79
Tot.	82	115	197	20	68	88	93	79	172	62	81	143
TP/(TP+FN)	sensitivity		84%	sensitivity		75%	sensitivity		92%	sensitivity		88%
TN/(TN+FP)	specificity		91	specificity		93	specificity		88	specificity		92

7.7 Area Under ROC Curve (AUROC)

The area under ROC curve is associated with the discriminant power of a test, and it may be determined through numerical methods as trapezium rule or statistical methods, such as Concordance, Somers'D and Mann-Whitney.

The ROC curve is an information summary about the accuracy of a continuous predictor. However, sometimes it is intended to summarize the ROC curve. The most commonly used statistic to summarize a ROC curve is the area under the ROC curve (AUROC, or AUC), also referred to as *c-statistic*.

One of the issues leading to the necessity of calculating the area under the curve is whether a cutoff is randomly selected in the area of higher histograms and another one in the lower histograms, and what is the probability that the one chosen from the lower histograms presents a higher scoring value than the one chosen from the highest histograms?

The *match probability* measures how often predictions and results match. For example, if a pair of customers is selected at random, one with a high score as a good payer and another with a low score as a bad payer, it will be considered a *concordant pair*. If we randomly select a pair in which the high-score customer is a bad payer and the low-score customer a good payer, we say it is a *discordant pair*. Some pairs have the same score, and they are called identical pairs (or tied pairs).

For measurement purposes of that area, it seems that it is equal to the *match probability,* and theoretically it varies in the range of 0.5 to 1, though in practice it usually lies in the range of 0.6 to 0.9 for the scorecards. There are several algorithms that make this calculation possible, but SPSS or SAS statistical programs already produce this calculation by default whenever the *logistic regression* runs in the program. According to Anderson (2007, 207), there is a relationship between *c-statistic* and Gini coefficient, which is given by the expression:

$$c \approx \frac{(D+1)}{2}$$

[44]

For example, for a Gini coefficient (or Somer's D) of 52 percent, the AUROC, or *c-statistic,* would be approximately 76 percent.

Table 31. Data relative to the area under the curve (AUROC) for the independent variable v_co_scoring

Area under the curve

Variable (s) of test result: v_co_scoring

Área	Standard model	Asymptotic Sig[b]	Asymptotic 95% confidence interval	
			Lower limit	Upper limit
.929	.005	.000	.919	.938

The test result variable (s): v_co_scoring has at least one node between the positive real state group and the actual negative state group. Statistics can be biased.

a. under the assumption no parametric

b. null hypothesis: real area = 0.5

Figure 16. Variable of test result *v_co_scoring*.

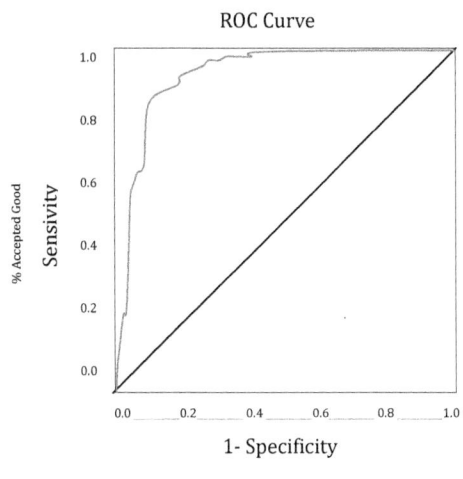

Table 32. Data relating to areas under the curves (AUROCs) for the variables v_co_scoring, v_co_credit_limit, v_co_current_balance

Area under the curve
Variable (s) of test result: v_co_scoring; v_co_credit_limit; v_co_current_balance

	Área	Standard model	Sig. asymptotic [b]	Asymptotic 95% confidence interval	
				Lower limit	Upper limit
v_co_scoring	.926	.010	.000	.906	.945
v_co_credit_limit	.928	.009	.000	.910	.945
v_co_current_balance	.849	.014	.000	.822	.875

a. under the assumption no parametric
b. null hypothesis: real area = 0.5

Figure 17. ROC curves of variables: *v_co_scoring*; *v_co_credit_limit* and *v_co_current_balance*.

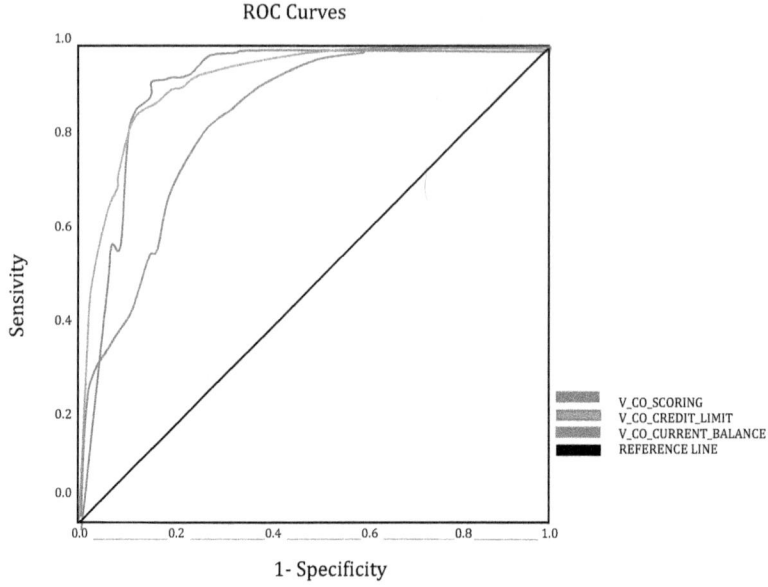

7.8 Type I and Type II Errors

We had the opportunity to explain the risk-manager decisions that motivated these errors (see sections 7.2 and 7.3). However, the risk manager may not be a person but a machine that makes decisions based on embedded data in statistical models. Thus, in the confusion matrix of our example, we found that the model hit 2,907 cases and failed 293. These classification errors take the designation of statistical type I and type II errors.

Table 33. Confusion matrix illustrating values obtained in the case study (chapter 8)

		Predicted classification by *logistic model*	
		Good ("1")	Bad ("0")
Current classification	Good ("1")	TP = 1474	FN= 167

	Observed	Bad ("0")	FP = 126	TN = 1433
		Total	TP+FP=1600	FN+TN =1600

Type I errors are those in which the model places a bad payer in the good payers group, and the type II errors place a good payer in the defaulting group. In the example, we can verify that 126 ratings are type I errors, and they are designated as false positive These classification errors represent 3.94 percent of the total sample (3,200).

Figure 18. Distribution curves of good and bad, illustrating the number of false positive (type I error).

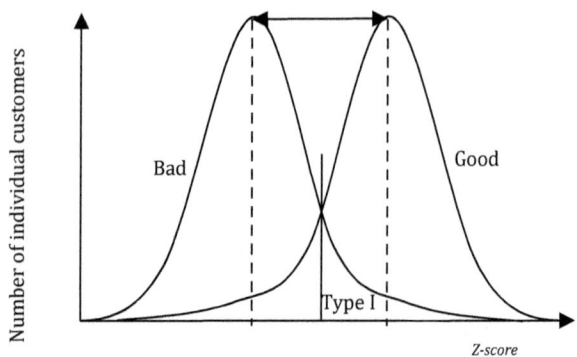

And 167 classification errors are type II, and they are called false negative These errors represent 5.22 percent of the total sample. The sum of the type I and type II errors is equal to 9.16 percent, and it translates the model error rate, meaning that the hit rate is 90.84 percent.

Figure 19. Distribution curves of good and bad, illustrating type II error.

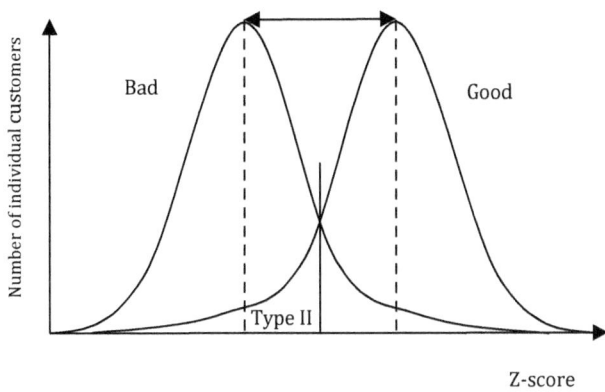

Figure 20. Distributions of good and bad illustrating the values obtained by application of the *logistic model* to the case study developed in chapter 8.

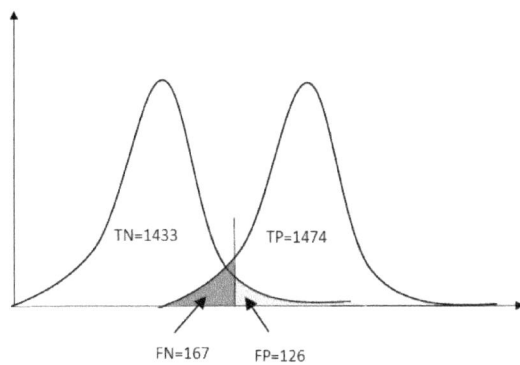

Table 34. SAS output illustrating data obtained by application of the *logistic model* to the case study developed in chapter 8

		OBSERVED		
		GOOD	BAD	Total
PREDICTED	GOOD	TP=1 474	FP=126	1 600
		46.06%	3.94%	50.00%
		PPV=92.13%	7.88%	
		Sensiv.=89.82%	8.08%	
	BAD	FN=167	TN=1 433	1 600
		5.22%	44.78%	50.00%
		10.44%	NPV=89.56%	
		10.18%	Specif.=91.92%	
	Total	1 641	1 559	3 200
		51.28%	48.72%	100.00%

In SAS output, we verify that, besides the abovementioned error percentages for the total sample. There is also the type I error rate, regarding the total number of observed bad customers (1,600), i.e., 7.88 percent, and type II error rate, with regard to the number of observed good customers (1,600) i.e., 10.44 percent. The formulas that translate these percentages are:

$$Type\ I\ Error\ Rate_{(Total\ Bad)} = \frac{FP}{TN + FN} = \frac{126}{1433 + 167} = 7.88\%$$

$$Type\ II\ Error\ Rate_{(Total\ Good)} = \frac{FN}{TP + FP} = \frac{167}{1474 + 126} = 10.44\%$$

Another criterion for identification of error rates, according to SAS, is to obtain type I error rate in relation to the ratio between FP and the sum of and type II error rate in relation to the ratio between the FN and the sum of FN + TP, in accordance with the following formulae:

$$Type\ I\ Error\ Rate = \frac{FP}{FP + TN} = \frac{126}{126 + 1433} = \frac{126}{1559} = 8.08\%$$

$$Type\ II\ Error\ Rate = \frac{FN}{FN + TP} = \frac{167}{167 + 1474} = \frac{167}{1641} = 10.18\%$$

Type I error rate is also referred to as *credit risk* and type II error rate as *commercial risk*. Such errors have consequences in terms of costs to the bank. In the first case, a loan was granted to a bad payer, and for that reason, it could cause a cost to the bank by the nonpayment of the obligation. In the second case, there is also a potential profit loss resulting from a loan to a good payer who has been refused credit.

Chapter 8

Case Study: Logistic-Regression Application to Revolving Credit

8.1 Methodology

The case study developed throughout this chapter was based on a job application of *logistic-regression* model to a database consisting of 4,000 credit-card users.

The aim of this study was to evaluate the robustness of the predictive *logistic model* in predicting the debt payment failure caused by the use of credit cards.

The criterion adopted in data collection followed the method proposed by several researchers, including Lewis (1992, 31), Mays (2001, 41), Siddiqi (2006, 70), and Anderson (2007, 260).

The process began by obtaining a sample that contained the same number of good and bad payers.

Thus, from the 4,000 credit-card users, 2,000 had a good-payer profile, and the other 2,000 had a bad-payer profile.

The second moment was based on dividing the sample of 4,000 credit-card users into two subsamples: one with 3,200 holders (1,600 good and 1,600 bad) and another sample with 800 (400 good and 400 bad).

The first sample, named as *in-sample* and containing 80 percent of all customers, was used to estimate the *logistic-model* parameters.

The second sample, called *out-of-sample* or *holdout sample* and containing the remaining 20 percent of users, served to validate *out o - sample* the results obtained by the first sample.

The third moment established criteria and methods for leading all the empirical research.

In this context, the dichotomous-dependent variable was created, designated as COD, taking value 1 when the model predicts a good account and 0 when it predicts a bad account.

The fourth moment was the *in-sample* characterization, using descriptive statistical measures to obtain more knowledge about the users who were part of the sample—in particular, their personal characteristics (age, gender, marital status, occupation, etc.) and other behavioral nature information caused by the experience the credit institution had already built on the individual (punctuality in payments, incidents, average balance, etc.).

On the fifth moment, the *logistic-regression* model was estimated using SPSS, E-Views, and SAS statistical programs, obtaining information about the model-prediction quality.

On the sixth moment, the model statistical validation was carried out through the *holdout sample,* which confirmed the predictive robustness of the previously estimated model.

The process allowed for finding a statistical model able to relate the probability of a credit-card user being good with his/her personal characteristics, while also including behavioral nature data.

8.2 Data Analysis

Among the characteristics relating to 4,000 credit-card users, 21 were identified as (wholly or partially) independent or explanatory variables of the *logistic-regression* model.

Some of these variables do not require any previous explanations (age, gender, income, etc.), although others require a preliminary clarification due to their more specific content.

One of the variables, designated as *scoring* (1), corresponds to a certain number of points (score) showing the credir card user position in a orthogonal reference frame, where in the abscissa it is shown his/her score, and in the ordinates it is shown the number of users in the portfolio.

This benchmark is very important because it is through it that we view frequency distributions of good and bad users and in which a border, known as *cutoff*, is established between them.

One of the statistical techniques to do this score is the *multivariate discriminant analysis* presented by Altman (1968), who designated it by *z-score* (see sections 2.3 and 2.4) and later the same author with Haldeman and Narayanam (1977), with the *Zeta* model.

Another variable concerns the maximum amount the user can pay with his/her credit card, designated as *credit limit* (2), also called *ceiling*.

This variable is calculated based on certain criteria, such as income, number of years in current job, marital status, liabilities in other credit institutions, etc.

The third variable refers to the value of the debt the user has in the final moment of the billing cycle, and it is designated as *current balance* (3).

The balance is calculated by the difference between total debt and total or partial amortizations made by the user to the financial institution on a monthly basis and on a specific date, with a given interest rate on that amount.

The fourth variable identifies the *state* (4) in which the account is being identified by a numeric code.

The fifth variable identifies the *code* (5) of the account classification, this ID being a combination with other various classifications.

The sixth variable identifies the remaining unpaid amount in the previous monthly statement, designated by *revolving* (6).

One of the other indicators measuring the account performance is its *profitability* (7), the seventh variable.

Other information identifies the *month* and the *year* to which the data refer, being presented in the format "yyyymm" (8).

The ninth variable is the classification code description (9).

The tenth variable gives the *code description* (10) of the *state* in which the account is.

The eleventh and twelfth variables report account *delinquency* in number of days.

The term *"delinquency"* has the meaning of "delay offence" in number of days exceeding the expiry date.

The remaining variables, ranging from the thirteenth to the twenty-first, do not require any explanations, such as gender (13), zip code (14), birth date (15), marital status (16), qualifications (17), geographical region (18), profession (19), age (20), and income (21), as we have already referred to these.

Table 35. Listing of independent variables of the sample used

1	v_co_scoring: behavioral scoring value concerning customer current account
2	v_co_credit_limit: (maximum amount the customer can spend using his credit card)
3	v_co_current_balance: current debt amount
4	ci_co_state: identifies the code of the state in which the account is
5	ci_co_class: identifies the account classification code (ci_co_state is a combination of various account classifications)
6	v_co_revolving: revolving amount i.e., the remaining unpaid amount
7	m_profitability: monthly profitable amount in the account
8	c_tp_month: identifies month to which relate data (format = yyyymm)
9	d_co_class: classification code description
10	d_co_state: state code description
11	delinq_60 days: delinquent account for more than 60 days old
12	delinq_90 days: delinquent account for more than 90 days old
13	gender (M/F)
14	cod_post-zip code
15	date of birth
16	marital status
17	academic qualifications
18	geographic region
19	profession
20	age
21	income

8.3 Distinction between Good and Bad Payers

The selection of 2,000 good payers and 2,000 bad payers followed a criteria with a certain number of parameters:

A good payer is the user who:

• has at least one active account in the past ten months;

• presents a maximum of one late payment in the last twelve months;

- had a maximum of one return in the last twelve months;
- presents "rfm" classes (recency, frequency and monetary), profitability, and revolving of four and five;
- in the last three months has an average account balance greater or equal to a given value, whose parameter can be adjusted according to other indicators, such as inflation;
- presents accounts under review with a noncompliance equal to or higher than sxity days in the last 2twenty-four months; and
- shows a turnover equal to or higher than a certain amount in the last three months. That value is determined on the basis of several criteria, including inflation and others with a commercial intent.

These were the seven main parameters considered for the good-payer classification.

A bad payer is the user who:

- introduces accounts at least once in default for more than a given number of days, in the last twenty-four months, with a balance equal to or higher than a given value;

- presents accounts three or more times in default for more than a given number of days, in the last twelve months, with a balance exceeding a certain value; and

- does not present any movement over a certain period of time, caused by prohibition of the use of the account or for other reasons.

8.4 Grouping of Variables According to Their Nature

The twenty-one variables were grouped into three categories: qualitative, quantitative, and dates, as shown in table 36:

Table 36. Grouping of independent variables according to their nature

Qualitative variables	Quantitative variables	Date variables
ci_co_state-identifies the state code in which the account is	v_co_scoring: behavioral scoring value concerning the customer current account.	Birth date
d_co_state - state code description	v_co_credit_limit: credit limit (maximum amount the customer can spend using his/her credit card).	c_tp_month-identifies the month to which data relate (format = yyyymm)
d_co_class: classification code description	v_co_current_balance: value of the current debt balance	
ci_co_class-identifies the account classification code (ci_co_state is a combination of various account classifications)	v_co_revolving: revolving amount, i.e. remaining unpaid value in the previous statement.	
delinq_60days -delinquent account for more than 60 days	m_profitability: monthly return value of the account	
delinq_90days -delinquent account for more than 90 days	age	
gender-(M/F)	income – net monthly remuneration	
Zip code		
marital status		
Qualifications: academic qualifications		
region-geographic region		
profession		

8.5 Variables Interpretation

Since the variables meaning may not be sufficiently clear, not only by abbreviations used but also by small detailed descriptions, we chose to interpret them using cross-tables.

8.5.1 Description vs. Account State ID

The first cross-tabulation was made between variable "*d_co_state,*" which means the code description of the account state, and variable "*ci_co_state*" identifying the code of the account state.

Table 37. Cross-table *ci_co_state* (identification code of the account state) and *d_co_state* (description of the account state)

Count			d_co_state			Total
			Active accounts	Nonactive accounts	Not-usable accounts	
ci_co_state	1		2602	0	0	2602
	2		0	281	0	281
	3		0	0	317	317
	Total		2602	281	317	3200

Now we can understand the meaning of those variables in which "*ci_co_state 1*" identifies active accounts, "*ci_co_state 2*" identifies nonactive accounts, and "*ci_co_state 3*" identifies unusable accounts.

From table 37, we note that 81 percent of customers belonging to the sample remain with their accounts active. If we now translate table 37 in a more complete way, it would appear as follows:

Table 38. Table 37 summary

Description	Identification code	Total	%
Active accounts	1	2602	81,3%
Nonactive accounts	2	281	8,8%
Not-usable accounts	3	317	9,9%
Total		3200	100,0 %

8.5.2 Description vs. Account Class ID

The same reasoning was applied to the account class, describing it via an identification code and its description. The description of the account class (*d_co_class*) and the identification code (*ci_co_class*) are presented in table 39:

Table 39. d_co_class and ci_co_class cross-table

ci_co_class * d_co_class Cross-tabulation

Count		d_co_class										Total
		A-Not fulfilled minimum-Balance <l.U.	C-2 months - balance < L.U.	D-3 months-balance<L.U.	E->=4 months-balance<L.U.	H-Balance>L.U.	I-1 month-balance>L.U.	J-2 months-balance>L.U.	K-3 months-balance>L.U.	L->=4 months-balance>L.U.	P-1 month-balance<L.U.	Without classification	
ci_co_class	0	34	0	0	0	0	0	0	0	0	0	0	34
	1	0	114	0	0	0	0	0	0	0	0	0	114
	2	0	0	55	0	0	0	0	0	0	0	0	55
	3	0	0	0	22	0	0	0	0	0	0	0	22
	6	0	0	0	0	16	0	0	0	0	0	0	16
	7	0	0	0	0	0	30	0	0	0	0	0	30
	8	0	0	0	0	0	0	0	27	0	0	0	27
	9	0	0	0	0	0	0	0	0	30	0	0	30
	13	0	0	0	0	0	0	0	0	0	256	0	256
	19	0	0	0	0	0	0	0	0	0	0	2577	2577
	20	0	0	0	0	0	0	39	0	0	0	0	39
Total		34	114	55	22	16	30	39	27	30	256	2577	3200

Table 39 was converted into table 40, and it shows that 80.5 percent of the accounts have the identification code 19, or "unrated," without comparing the balance with any other parameter.

Table 40. Table 39 summary

Description	Id	Quantity	Meaning
A	0	34	Not fulfilled minimum-Balance < l. U
C	1	114	2 Months-Balance < L.U.
D	2	55	3 Months-Balance < l. U
E	3	22	> = 4 Months-Balance < l. U
H	6	16	Balance > L.U.
I	7	30	1 Month-Balance > L.U.
J	20	39	2 Months-Balance > L.U.
K	8	27	3 Months-Balance > L.U.
L	9	30	> = 4 Months-Balance > l. U
P	13	256	1 Month-Balance < L.U.
S/C	19	2577	Unrated
Total		3200	

8.5.3 Overdue Accounts for More than Sixty Days vs. Ninety Days

Delinquent accounts are those that, at any given time, have shown a certain payment delay in relation to the maturity date.

In the cross-table (table 41), we can note the following: of the 3,200 accounts that exceeded expiry date at least for sixty days, 2,913 were bad accounts, and 287 were good accounts. From the accounts exceeding ninety days, 3,066 were bad accounts, and 134 were good.

Table 41. Data crossing with different aging balances

delinq_90 days * delinq_60 days Cross-tabulation					
Count			Delinq_60 days		
			0	1	Total
Delinq_90 days		0	2913	153	3066
		1	0	134	134
	Total		2913	287	3200

What conclusions can we draw from the analysis of these numbers? The answer is simple: there was a worsening of the aging of bad accounts balance and an improvement in the good accounts during that period of one month.

For the 2,913 bad accounts with a sixty-day late payment, there were more than 153 accounts exceeding ninety days, totaling 3,066 accounts (3066-2913 = 153).

In the 287 good accounts that had reached the age of sixty days, there was a decrease of 153 accounts, because only 134 accounts surpassed ninety days (287-153 = 134), therefore, an improvement of 153 cases (287-134 = 153).

As mentioned in section 8.1, this fourth moment of the study is intended to obtain a more detailed and clarifying knowledge about the differences between good and bad accounts, allowing a more clear understanding of the behavior of explanatory variables, which will be subsequently analyzed by the *logistic model*, the next phase of this research process.

8.5.4 Gender

Table 42. Frequency table by gender
Gender * COD cross-tabulation

		COD 0	COD 1	Total
Gender	F	553	398	951
	M	1047	1202	2249
Total		1600	1600	3200

Table 42 stresses the large difference between the number of male users (70.3 percent) (2,249/3,200) and female users (29.7 percent) (951/3,200).

When questioning the financial institution about the reasons that would justify this disparity, we learned that this is a pseudo anomaly, because all male married users automatically receive another card assigned to their wives, although both cards have the same ID.

As for noncompliance, table 42 shows that 34.6 percent (553/1,600) are female, and 65.4 percent (1,047/1,600) are male. From the checked percentage, we cannot conclude that men are the worst payers since the number of men and women belonging to the sample is not the same.

If women represent 29.7 percent of the sample (951/3,200), as seen in table 42, and are responsible for 34.6 percent of noncompliance (553/1,600), it means that, in proportion, they are worse payers than men. They accounts for 70.3 percent of the sample (2,249/3,200), but they are responsible for 65.4 percent of noncompliance (1,047/1,600), which is, in proportion, a lower percentage.

With regard to fulfillment, table 42 shows that 24.9 percent (398/1,600) are women, and 75.1 percent (1,202/1,600) are men. From this analysis, we can conclude that men are, in statistical terms (in this sample and in this context), more compliant than women.

8.5.5 Marital Status

Table 43. Values of different marital-status attributes

In table 43, there are the marital-status attributes of good and bad payers rated by gender.

Gender			Marital status												
			Widowed		Married		Divorced		Separated		Single		Unanswered		Total
F	COD	0	23	4.2%	208	37.6%	66	11.9%	3	0.5%	87	15.7%	166	30.0%	553	100.0%
		1	25	6.3%	219	55.0%	68	17.1%	2	0.5%	52	13.1%	32	8.0%	398	100.0%
		Sub Tot.	48	5.0%	427	44.9%	134	14.1%	5	0.5%	139	14.6%	198	20.8%	951	100.0%
M	COD	0	7	0.7%	514	49.1%	61	5.8%	5	0.5%	108	10.3%	352	33.6%	1047	100.0%
		1	20	1.7%	918	76.4%	93	7.7%	6	0.5%	59	4.9%	106	8.8%	1202	100.0%
		Sub Tot.	27	1.2%	1432	63.7%	154	6.8%	11	0.5%	167	7.4%	458	20.4%	2249	100.0%
		Total	75	2.34%	1859	58.1%	288	9.0%	16	0.5%	306	9.6%	656	20.5%	3200	100.0%

When we analyzed the variable gender according to good and bad account classification in section 8.5.4, we found that, among women, 58.1 percent are bad payers (553/951) against 46.6 percent among men (1,047/2,249).

However, in table 43, there was a reversal of this trend in married women, who are 37.6 percent of bad accounts against 49.1 percent of married men. In all other marital status, women have a higher percentage of bad payers than men, with the exception of unanswered. Divorced and single women have an higher percentage of bad accounts than divorced and single men (11.9 and 15.7 percent versus 5.8 and 10.3 percent, respectively). Women who did not answer represent 30 percent of bad accounts against 33.6 percent of men. Among those widowed, women also have a higher percentage of bad accounts *versus* men. In analyzing these results to better understand what is the phenomenon leading the married woman to a be better payer than the married man, we empirically checked a possible reason for this reversal. When opening an account for a married man, the financial institution issues another card with the same account number for his wife. When she uses her card and fails to comply with the payments on the due date, the noncompliance is recorded in her husband's account. So married men, even if they do not use their credit cards, statistically aggravate their credibility (creditworthiness).

Table 44. Marital status by gender and frequency by code (2)

			\multicolumn{12}{c	}{Marital status}	
			\multicolumn{2}{c	}{Widowed}	\multicolumn{2}{c	}{Married}	\multicolumn{2}{c	}{Divorced}	\multicolumn{2}{c	}{Separated}	\multicolumn{2}{c	}{Single}	\multicolumn{2}{c	}{Unanswered}	
F	COD	0	23	47.9%	208	48.7%	66	49.3%	3	60.0%	87	62.6%	166	83.8%	553
		1	25	52.1%	219	51.3%	68	50.7%	2	40.0%	52	37.4%	32	16.2%	398
	Total		48	100.0%	427	100.0%	134	100.0%	5	100.0%	139	100.0%	198	100.0%	951
M	COD	0	7	25.9%	514	35.9%	61	39.6%	5	45.5%	108	64.7%	352	76.9%	104
		1	20	74.1%	918	64.1%	93	60.4%	6	54.5%	59	35.3%	106	23.1%	120
	Total		27	100,0%	1432	100.0%	154	100-.0%	11	100-.0%	167	100.0%	458	100.0%	224

Figure 21. Marital status by gender and frequency by code.

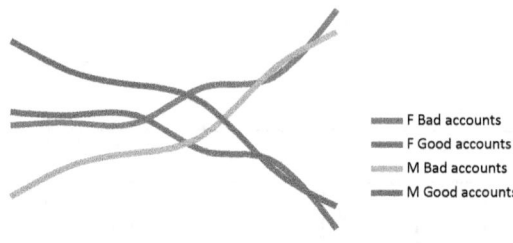

8.5.6 Behavioral Scoring Scale for the User-Current Account (v_co_scoring)

Table 45 groups the number of accounts of good and bad payers by score ranges:

Table 45. Frequencies of good and bad by score ranges

Score	Good	Bad
4-300	1	1
301-305	0	1
306-310	0	2
311-315	0	6
316-320	0	3
321-325	0	9
326-330	0	13
331-335	0	11
336-340	0	24
341-345	0	12
346-350	0	5
351-355	0	5
356-362	0	3
363-599	0	35
600-605	0	1
606-610	0	33
611-615	0	17
616-620	0	36
621-625	0	53
626-630	0	101
631-635	0	31
636-640	0	54
641-645	0	32
646-650	0	76
651-655	0	69
656-660	0	76
661-665	0	94
666-670	0	94
671-675	3	87
676-680	5	95
681-685	8	100
686-690	9	130
691-695	21	130
696-700	82	115
701-705	20	68
706-710	93	79
711-715	62	81
716-720	401	64
721-725	47	34
726-730	708	63
731-735	128	17
736-740	218	23
741-745	113	12
746-750	56	3
751-755	3	0
756-760	22	2
765-770	0	0
	2000	2000

8.5.7 Credit Limit

Credit limit (ceiling) is the maximum amount the customer can use with his/her card (v_co_credit_limit).

To analyze the relationship between the *scoring* variable and the *credit-limit* variable, we have built the following scatter diagram:

Figure 22. Scatter diagram showing the spatial positioning of good and bad users when crossing *credit limit* of the account with the respective *scoring* position.

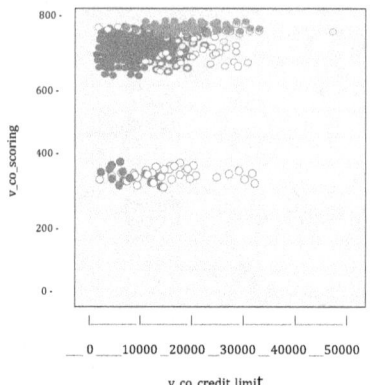

Figure 22 offers the following explanations and comments:

8.5.7.1: Dispersion of good and bad customers is made at credit-limit level ranging from 0 € to 50,000 €.

8.5.7.2: Scoring break among the higher levels (700 to 770 points) has Good and Bad customers, what is according to what Table 45 has shown.

8.5.7.3: In the range between 200 and 400 in the *v_co_scoring* ordinate, there is a set of bad payers. According to information from the financial institution, this account set refers to prelitigation, litigation, or other special situations.

8.5.8: Current account balance (*v_co_current_balance*) is the debt amount on the observation date (the end of the billing cycle).

8.5.9: Revo*lving* is the remaining unpaid amount in the previous account statement (*v_co_revolving*).

8.5.10: Profitability is the amount of account profitability (*m_profitability*).

8.5.11: Sample customers, on the date was obtained, had an average age of fifty-fve years (table 46 and figure 24).

Table 46. Descriptive statistics of characteristic age

Descriptive statistics

	N	Minimum	Maximum	Mean	Std. deviation
Age	3200	24	93	54.64	10.066
Valid N (listwise)	3200				

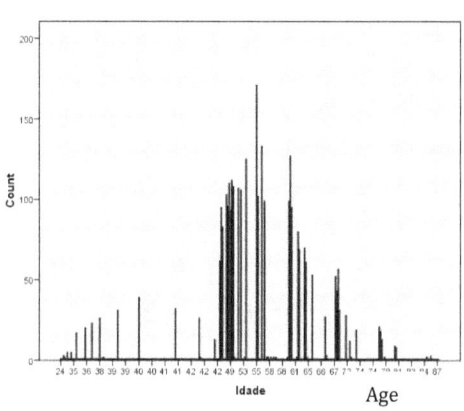

Figure 24. Frequencies of sample users' age.

Table 47. Frequencies of different types of academic qualifications

Academic qualifications

		Frequency	Percent	Valid Percent	Cumulative Percent
Valid	12th grade	21	.7	.7	.7
	Middle School	9	.3	.3	.9
	Higher Education/Degree/Masters	329	10.3	10.3	11.2
	Compulsory schooling	12	.4	.4	11.6
	Less than compulsory education	4	.1	.1	11.7
	Other	1727	54.0	54.0	65.7
	No Answer	1098	34.3	34.3	100.0
	Total	3200	100.0	100.0	

8.5.12: Academic qualifications (*qualific_d*)

8.5.13: Income, or net monthly income

This characteristic was not considered in the model because it showed an income value, in the vast majority of cases, equal to 0. Other variables—such as zip code, geographic region, occupation, date of birth, and date of the month to which the data relate—did not deserve additional explanations.

The following procedure consisted in transforming some of the qualitative variables in fictitious quantitative variables (dummies).

This transformation was made manually, rather than by the SPSS statistical program making choices that could counteract the good sense imposed by reality.

This topic will be developed in section 8.6.

8.6 Data Transformation

To make it easier for the interpretation of the estimates for some of the qualitative variables coefficients, they were transformed into fictitious numeric variables (dummy variables). The transformation of variables is made according to a dichotomization of the attributes, as shown in table 48.

Table 48. Frequencies of categorical variables by code

Categorical variables codings			
		Frequency	Parameter coding
Qualific (dummy)	0	2825	0
	1	375	1
ci_co_class (dummy)	0	2577	0
	1	623	1
d_co_class (dummy)	0	3058	0
	1	142	1
d_co_state (dummy)	0	2602	0
	1	598	1
Gender (dummy)	0	2249	0
	1	951	1
Region (dummy)	0	2310	0
	1	890	1
Marital status (dummy)	0	1859	0
	1	1341	1
ci_co_state (dummy)	0	2602	0
	1	598	1

The criterion followed for the assignment of codes 0 and 1 was to consider the attributes containing the largest number of observations (Anderson 2007, 359) as 0, as shown in tables 48 and 49.

Table 49. Frequency of attributes by reference and answer categories

	Attributes	Frequency	Control group	Treatment group
			0	1
Geographic region	Alentejo	135		1
	Algarve	158		1
	Beira Interior	30		1
	Centro	168		1
	Ilhas	136		1
	Lisboa	1063	0	
	Lisboa Cidade	749	0	
	Litoral	211		1
	Norte	52		1
	Porto	342	0	
	Porto Cidade	156	0	
	0	34		1
	1	114		1
	2	55		1

	3	22		1
	6	16		1
	7	30		1
	8	27		1
	9	30		1
	13	256		1
	19	**2577**	0	
	20	39		1
d_co_class	Unfullfilled minimum-balance < l. U	34		1
	2 Months-balance < L.U.	114		1
	3 Months-balance < l. U	55		1
	> = 4 Months-balance < l. U	22		1
	Balance > L.U.	16		1
	1 Month-balance > L.U.	30		1
	2 Months-balance > L.U.	39		1
	3 Months-balance > L.U.	27		1
	> = 4 Months-balance > l. U	30		1
	1 Month-balance < L.U.	256		1
	Unrated	**2577**	0	
Academic qualifications	12th grade	21		1
	Middle school	9		1
	Higher education/degree/masters	329		1
	Compulsory schooling	12		1
	Less than compulsory education	4		1
	Other	**1727**	0	
	Unanswered	1098		1
Marital status	**Married**	**1859**	0	
	Divorced	288		1
	Unanswered	656		1
	Separated	16		1
	Single	306		1
	Widowed	75		1
ci_co_state	**1**	**2602**	0	
	2	281		1
	3	317		1
Gender	F	951		1
	M	**2249**	0	
d_co_state	**Active accounts**	**2602**	0	
	Nonactive acc./ Not-usable acc.	598		1

The way the categories are codified will determine the direction of the *odds* ratios, as well as the estimates for the coefficients (Tabachnick and Fidell 2007, 464). SPSS and E-Views programs give the estimated equation for the probability of the dependent variable being equal to 1, while the SAS program solves the equation for the category codified as 0. In other words, an *odds* ratio of four in SPSS represents, for example, a ratio of 80 percent of good payers and 20 percent of bad payers), but if the program used is SAS (SAS Institute Inc.), the *odds* ratio will be 0.25 (ratio of 20 percent of bad payers and 80 percent of good payers).

For a better interpretation, we use the disease dichotomy as the answer category codified as 1 and health as the reference category codified as 0. In the previous table, we have given the example of the *d_co_state* variable whose attributes are active accounts (healthy) codified as reference category (0) and nonactive accounts/not-usable accounts (sick) codified as answer category (1).

8.7 Variables Characterization by Descriptive Statistics Measures

For a better characterization of the variables, in terms of descriptive statistics, we present tables 50 and 51.

Table 50. Univariate statistical measures

	\multicolumn{7}{c|}{Univariate statistics}						
				\multicolumn{2}{c	}{Missing}	\multicolumn{2}{c	}{No. of extremes[a]}
	N	Mean	Std. deviation	Count	Percent	Low	High
v_co_scoring	3200	686.33	82.832	0	.0	137	0
v_co_credit_limit	3200	8678.06	6957.993	0	.0	0	110
v_co_current_balance	3200	4283.3460	4303.24032	0	.0	0	186
v_co_revolving	3200	3618.3288	3809.90513	0	.0	0	176
m_profitability	3200	66.4332	77.21507	0	.0	0	156
ci_co_state dummy	3200	.19	.390	0	.0	0	598
ci_co_class dummy	3200	.19	.396	0	.0	0	623
d_co_class dummy	3200	.19	.396	0	.0	0	623
d_co_state dummy	3200	.19	.390	0	.0	0	598
delinq_60days	3200	.09	.286	0	.0	0	287
delinq_90days	3200	.04	.200	0	.0	0	134
Gender dummy	3200	.30	.457	0	.0	0	0
Marital status dummy	3200	.42	.493	0	.0	0	0
Region dummy	3200	.28	.448	0	.0	0	0
Income	3200	185.90	925.187	0	.0	0	103
Qualific. dummy	3200	.46	.499	0	.0	0	0
Age	3200	54.98	10.173	0	.0	22	97
ci_co_state	3200	1.29	.634	0	.0	0	317
ci_co_class	3200	16.92	4.984	0	.0	241	0
c_tp_month	3200	200706.00	.000	0	.0	.	.

a. Number of cases outside the range (Mean - 2*SD, Mean + 2*SD).

Table 51. Statistical descriptive measures of independent variables

						\multicolumn{2}{c	}{Descriptives}		
						\multicolumn{2}{c	}{95% Confidence interval for mean}		
		N	Mean	Std. deviation	Std. error	Lower bound	Upper bound	Minimum	Maximum
v_co_scoring	0	1600	643.17	107.297	2.682	637.91	648.43	4	756
	1	1600	725.23	22.656	.566	724.12	726.34	4	762
	Total	3200	684.20	87.722	1.551	681.16	687.24	4	762
v_co_credit_limit	0	1600	4779.66	3906.821	97.671	4588.09	4971.24	500	25000
	1	1600	14549.75	6241.813	156.045	14243.67	14855.82	452	50000
	Total	3200	9664.71	7139.633	126.212	9417.24	9912.17	452	50000

v_co_current_balance	0	1600	2909.563125	3.2349773E3	80.8744331	2750.932075	3068.194175	-292.0000	27742.0000
	1	1600	6475.208125	5.0623481E3	126.5587015	6226.969726	6723.446524	-2815.0000	30464.0000
	Total	3200	4692.385625	4.6065205E3	81.4325478	4532.720354	4852.050896	-2815.0000	30464.0000
v_co_revolving	0	1600	2597.038125	2.9586205E3	73.9655136	2451.958566	2742.117684	.0000	25926.0000
	1	1600	5350.391875	4.5895978E3	114.7399456	5125.335360	5575.448390	.0000	27796.0000
	Total	3200	3973.715000	4.0987917E3	72.4570843	3831.647973	4115.782027	.0000	27796.0000
m_profitability	0	1600	48.3644	65.14222	1.62856	45.1700	51.5587	-14.00	1585.00
	1	1600	96.7456	86.68579	2.16714	92.4949	100.9964	-67.00	497.00
	Total	3200	72.5550	80.38967	1.42110	69.7686	75.3414	-67.00	1585.00
Age	0	1600	51.666875	9.2238320	.2305958	51.214573	52.119177	30.0000	87.0000
	1	1600	58.963750	9.1679451	.2291986	58.514189	59.413311	35.0000	89.0000
	Total	3200	55.315312	9.8921166	.1748696	54.972445	55.658180	30.0000	89.0000
Gender dummy	0	1600	.30	.460	.012	.28	.33	0	1
	1	1600	.21	.407	.010	.19	.23	0	1
	Total	3200	.26	.437	.008	.24	.27	0	1
Marit.-status dummy	0	1600	.48	.500	.012	.46	.51	0	1
	1	1600	.26	.437	.011	.24	.28	0	1
	Total	3200	.37	.483	.009	.35	.39	0	1
Qualific. dummy	0	1600	.12	.326	.008	.10	.14	0	1
	1	1600	.15	.353	.009	.13	.16	0	1
	Total	3200	.13	.340	.006	.12	.14	0	1
ci_co_classDummy	0	1600	.42	.493	.012	.39	.44	0	1
	1	1600	.01	.111	.003	.01	.02	0	1
	Total	3200	.21	.411	.007	.20	.23	0	1

In table 50, we see that the *logistic model* will not be negatively affected by *missings,* and in table 51, an observation of minimum and maximum values ensures that the *logistic model* will also not be negatively affected by *outliers.*

8.8 Application of Logit Model to Sample Data

To analyze the relationship between the probability of a customer being a good payer and his/her personal characteristics, including account data, we use the *logit* model, whose parameters were estimated from E-Views.

As a dependent variable, we considered the COD variable, which assumes values 0 and 1 for bad and good payers, respectively.

As independent variables, we initially considered fourteen variables, as shown in table 52.

Table 52. Fourteen independent variables initially considered in the model

1	v_co_scoring
2	v_co_credit_limit
3	v_co-current_balance
4	v_co_revolving
5	delinq_60days
6	delinq_90days
7	m_profitability
8	age
9	ci_co_state (Dummy)
10	ci_co_class (Dummy)
11	gender (Dummy)
12	marital_status (Dummy)
13	region (Dummy)
14	qualific. (Dummy)

The results obtained directly from E-Views are presented in the tables of the following subsection.

8.8.1 Model Application to In-Sample Data

As a starting point, we included all the explanatory variables initially considered in the template. In a second step, and following the principle of parsimony, we excluded variables whose estimated coefficients proved as not statistically significant at a significance level of 10 percent. The excluded variables were:

Table 53. Variables excluded from the logistic model as not statiscally significant

1	ci_co_state (Dummy)
2	delinq_60days
3	delinq_90days
4	region(Dummy)

The estimation results are shown in table 54.

Table 54. Explanatory variables remaining in the model after excluding variables whose estimated coefficients proved not to be statistically significant

Dependent variable: COD
Method: ML - binary logit (Quadratic hill climbing)
Sample 1: 3,200
Included observations: 3,200
Convergence achieved after 23 iterations
Covariance matrix computed using second derivatives

Variable	Coefficient	Std. error	z-statistic	Prob.
V_CO_SCORING	0.066500	0.003795	17.52427	0.0000
V_CO_CREDIT_LIMIT	0.000621	2.05E-05	12.74539	0.0000
V_CO_CURRENT_BALANCE	0.000499	0.000110	4.52673	0.0000
M_PROFITABILITY	-0.008396	0.002934	-2.861424	0.0042
AGE	0.018678	0.007091	2.634029	0.0084
QUALIFIC_D	-0.602927	0.132102	-4.564096	0.0000
CI_CO_CLASS_D	-1.43407	0.349123	-4.107634	0.0000
V_CO_REVOLVING	-0.000384	0.000120	-3.201036	0.0014
MARITAL_STATUS_D	-0.578892	0.134513	-4.303619	0.0000
GENDER_D	0.808648	0.14411	5.599634	0.0000
C	-49.89290	2.752544	-18.12610	0.0000
McFadden R-squared	0.653876	Mean dependent var		0.500000
S.D. dependent var	0.500078	S.E. of regression		0.260019
Akaike info criterion	0.486704	Sum squared resid		-767.7269
Schwartz criterion	0.507573	Log likelihood		-2218.071
Hannan-Quinn criter.	0.494186	Restr.log likelihood		-0.239915
LR statistic	2.900.688	Avg.log likelihood		
Prob(LR statistic)	0.000000			
Obs with Dep=0	1600	Total obs		3200
Obs with Dep=1	1600			

8.8.2 Quality Evaluation of the Adjustment

To conclude on the goodness of fit for the *in-sample*, we started by analyzing some of the previous results.

The model is globally valid because it rejects the null hypothesis in the likelihood-test ratio ; see section 5.2) that compares *log likelihood* of two models, *with* and *without* explanatory variables:

$$[-2LLF_\emptyset (initial\ or\ baseline) - (-2LLF_1(final\ or\ full\ model)]$$

Since the probability associated with the LR test (0.0000) is clearly lower than the conventionally used significance levels, there is at least *one* estimated coefficient statistically significant. This means that there is at least one explanatory variable whose variation is statistically related to the probability of a customer being a good payer.

Therefore, the model with all the explanatory variables shows better predictions than those resulting from the model only with a constant (*c*).

The estimated coefficients β are all statistically significant, given the value and the probability associated with Z tests. This means all the explanatory variables are statistically relevant to describe the probability of COD variable being equal to 1 (the good payer).

Table 54 also gives information about the contribution or importance of each one of the explanatory variables.

Estimates for coefficients β (see the second column in table 54) are the values used in the logistic-distribution function to estimate the probability of a customer being a good payer.

We verify that there are positive and negative estimates that indicate the direction of the relationship between the explanatory variables and the dependent variable, i.e., how the variation in one of the explanatory variables affects, in average terms, the probability of the customer being a good payer.

Thus, negative values indicate that, on average, an increase in explanatory variable will result in the decreased probability of the customer being a good payer. This is the case of variables: *m_profitability, qualific_dummy, ci_co_class_dummy, v_co_revolving,* and *marital_status_dummy.*

Positive values show that, on average, an increase in the explanatory variable will result in the increased probability of the customer being a good payer. This is the case of the variables: *v_co_scoring, v_co_credit_limit, v_co_current_balance, age,* and *gender_dummy.*

When referring to the impact of the explanatory variables on the probability of the dependent variable being equal to 1, we usually calculate the exponential estimate for each of the coefficients. The resulting values are estimates of *odds* ratios for each of the independent variables. *Odds ratios* represent the expected variation (increase or decrease if the ratio is less than 1) on the dependent variable when the value of the independent variable varies one unit.

McFadden's R^2 value is 0.65, which means that there is a significant increase in the maximum value of the *log-likelihood function* when all explanatory variables are considered in relation to the model that only includes the *constant* (c).

Beyond the *logit* model, *probit* and *gompit* models were also estimated (based on normal standard distributions and type I extreme values, respectively). To conclude which of the models is best suited to describe the data-generator process, the Vuong test (1989) allows for comparing "nonnested" models[3] in a functional form, as there are the cases of *logit, probit,* and *gompit* models.

Three tests were performed, considering in null hypothesis H_0 each one of the previous models (*logit, probit,* and *gompit*) and in alternative hypothesis H_1, each one of the two other models.

Test 1: H_0 : *logit* Model, H_1: *probit* model

Test 2: H_0: *logit* Model, H_1: *gompit* model

Test 3: H_0: *probit* Model, H_1: *gompit* model

The results obtained were as follows:

Table 55. Vuong test results

	Test 1	Test 2	Test 3
Vuong	2.73	-0.72	-1.76

Since the value of test 1 falls on the positive part of the critical region (for a significance level of 0.05, the critical value of the standardized normal distribution in a bilateral test is approximately 2), we concluded that the *logit* model is more appropriate than the *probit* model to describe the generating process of the data constituting the sample. According to the result of tests 2 and 3, and

---

[3] Two models are called "nonnested" when it is impossible to present a model as a specific case of another one, imposing restrictions to certain parameters of the more general model. Models can also be "nonnested" regarding functional relationship and error structures.

since we do not reject the null hypothesis (H_0), the differences in the maximum value of the *log-likelihood function* (LLF_{Max}) are not statistically significant between *logit* and *gompit* models or between the *probit* and *gompit* models.

Therefore, regarding Vuong test results, and considering the superiority of the *logit* model over *probit* model, it was decided to proceed with the analysis of the *logistic-regression* results. To conclude on the goodness of fit, we can still build a summary table with the customers' classification. If the estimated probability resulting from the model is equal to or less than 0.5 (value considered by default), the customer is classified as a bad payer. Otherwise, we consider $Y = 1$; that is, the customer is a good payer. The results obtained are shown in table 56.

Table 56. E-Views output related to *in-sample* data showing the general hit rate of 90,84 percent

Expectation-prediction evaluation for binary specification
Success cutoff C=0.5

	Estimated equation			Constant probability		
	Dep= 0	Dep= 1	Total	Dep= 0	Dep= 1	Total
P(Dep= 1)<=C	1433	126	1559	1600	1600	3200
P(Dep=1)>C	167	1474	1641	0	0	0
Total	1600	1600	3200	1600	1600	3200
Correct	1433	1474	2907	1600	0	1600
% Correct	89.56	92.13	90.84	100	0	50
% Incorrect	10.44	7.87	9.16	0	100	50
Total Gain	-10,44	92.13	40.84			
Percent Gain	NA	92.13	81.69			
	Estimated equation			Constant probability		
	Dep= 0	Dep= 1	Total	Dep= 0	Dep= 1	Total
E(#of Dep= 0)	1374.32	226.03	1600.36	800.00	800.00	1600.00
E(#of Dep= 1)	225.68	1373.97	1599.64	800.00	800.00	1600.00
Total	1600.00	1600.00	3200.00	1600.00	1600.00	3200.00
Correct	1374.32	1373.97	2748.29	800.00	800.00	1600.00
% Correct	85.90	85.87	85.88	50.00	50.00	50.00
% Incorrect	14.10	14.13	14.12	50.00	50.00	50.00
Total Gain*	35.90	35.87	35.88			
Percent Gain	71.79	71.75	71.77			

*Change in" % correct" from default (constant probability) specification
**Percent of incorrect (default) prediction corrected by equation

Information given in table 56 is summarized in table 57.

Table 57. Final classification table of *in-sample*

Classification table [a]					
			Predicted		
			COD		
			0	1	Percentage correct
Observed	COD	0	1433	126	89,56
		1	167	1474	92,13
		Overall percentage			90,84
a. The cut value is, 500					

8.8.3 Marginal Effects of the Explanatory Variables on the Probability of a User Being a Good Payer

The direct interpretation of the coefficients is sometimes complex since, in a model with a binary-dependent variable, the estimates for the coefficients cannot be directly interpreted as the marginal effect of each one of the explanatory variables on the dependent variable (except for the linear probabilistic model). The marginal effect of explanatory variable X_j in relation to the probability of $Y = 1$ is the product of the density function of logistic probability by estimating its associated coefficient. A procedure suggested by several authors (Greene 2002) is to evaluate the marginal effect for each observation and to consider the average of marginal individual effects. When it comes to a dummy variable, and because it is not a continuous variable, the above procedure is not the most appropriate to calculate the respective marginal effect. In this case, we choose to calculate the difference in estimated probabilities resulting from *Dummy=1* and *Dummy=0* at the midpoint of the remaining explanatory variables. These are the two procedures at the base of the results presented in table 58.

Table 58. Marginal effects

v_co_scoring	0.004906
v_co_credit_limit	0.000019
v_co_current_balance	0.000037
m_profitability	-0.000619
age	0.001378
qualific_d	-0.114342
ci_co_class_d	-0.217117
v_co_revolving	-0.000028
marital_status_d	-0.110437
gender_d	0.193188

Table 59. Frequencies of good and bad for the characteristic *Qualific_Dummy*

V_CO_SCORING	0.004906	On average, for every variation of a unit in v_co_scoring, the probability of the customer being a Good payer varies 0.004906 in the same direction, assuming everything else is constant.
V_CO_CREDIT_LIMIT	0.000019	On average, for every variation of a unit in v_co_credit_limit, the probability of the customer being a Good payer varies 0.000019 in the same direction, assuming everything else is constant.
V_CO_CURRENT_BALANCE	0.000037	On average, for every variation of a unit in v_co_current_balance, the probability of the customer being a Good payer varies 0.000037 in the same direction, assuming everything else is constant.
M_PROFITABILITY	-0.000619	On average, for every variation of a unit in m_profitability, the probability of the customer being a Good payer varies 0.000619 in reverse order, assuming everything else is constant.
AGE	0.001378	On average, for every variation of a unit in age, the probability of the customer being a Good payer varies 0.001378 in the same direction, assuming everything else is constant.
QUALIFIC_D	-0.114342	On average, the probability of a customer belonging to the Category "Answer" being a Good payer is lower at 0.114342 to the same probability of customers belonging to the category "Reference," assuming everything else is constant.
CI_CO_CLASS_D	-0.217117	On average, the probability of a customer belonging to the Category "Answer" being a Good payer is lower at 0.217117 to the same probability of customers belonging to the category "Reference," assuming everything else is constant
V_CO_REVOLVING	-0.000028	On average, for every variation of a unit in v_co_revolving, the probability of the customer being a Good payer varies 0.000028 in reverse order, assuming everything else is constant.
MARITAL_STATUS_D	-0.110437	On average, the probability of a customer belonging to the Category "Answer" being a Good payer is lower at 0.110437 to the same probability of customers belonging to the category "Reference" (Married), assuming everything else is constant.
GENDER_D	0.193188	On average, the probability of a man being a Good payer is higher at 0.193188 to the same probability of women, assuming everything else is constant.

			Parameter coding
		Frequency	(1)
Qualific_Dummy	0	1727	0
	1	1473	1

Table 60. *Qualific* characteristics by reference and answer categories

Charact.	Attributes	Freq.	Reference control group category	Answer treatment group category
			0	1
Academic Qualif.	12th grade	21		1
	Middle School	9		1
	Higher Education/Degree/Masters	329		1
	Compulsory schooling	12		1
	Less than the compulsory education	4		1
	Other	1727	0	
	Unanswered	1098		1

Table 61. Frequency of bad and good accounts of independent variable *ci_co_class*

Categorial variables coding				
				Parameter coding
			Frequency	(1)
ci_co_class(Dummy)		0	2577	0
		1	623	1

Table 62. Frequency of attributes of characteristic *ci_co_class*

Characteristic	Attributes	Frequency	Reference control group category	Answer treatment group category
			0	1
ci_co_class	0	34		1
	1	114		1
	2	55		1
	3	22		1
	6	16		1
	7	30		1
	8	27		1
	9	30		1
	13	256		1
	19	2577	0	
	20	39		1

Table 63. Frequency of bad and good accounts of independent variable marital status (*dummy*)

Categorial variables coding				
				Parameter coding
			Frequency	(1)
Marital status (dummy)		0	1859	0
		1	1341	1

Table 64. Frequency of attributes of *marital-status* characteristic

Characteristic	Attributes	Frequency	Reference control group category	Answer treatment group category
			0	1
Marital status	Married	1859	0	
	Divorced	288		1
	Unanswered	656		1
	Separated	16		1
	Single	306		1
	Widowed	75		1

Table 65. Frequency of attributes of characteristic gender

Characteristic	Attributes	Frequency	Reference control group category	Answer treatment group category
			0	1
Gender	F	951		1
	M	2249	0	

8.8.4 Heteroscedasticity Errors Test

Heteroscedasticity is considered a serious problem in models with a binary-dependent variable, because if the variance of errors is not constant, the estimators for the coefficients are no longer the most efficient. To conclude on the homoscedasticity of errors, we have estimated the value of the *LM* (Lagrange Multiplier) test proposed by Davidson and MacKinnon (1993), assuming *v_co_credit_limit* [4] is the variable responsible for heteroscedasticity.

The *LM* test statistic is the *Explained Sum of Squares* (*ESS*) of auxiliary regression, whose dependent variables are the standardized residues of *logistic regression*, and it has a chi-square distribution with "x" degrees of freedom (*df*), where "x" is the number of variables considered to explain heteroscedasticity. In this case, $df=1$, which is corresponded by a critical value of 3.84.

To calculate the test value, we used the methodology of Davidson and MacKinnon (1993), and we followed directly to E-Views, having obtained the value $ESS=37.82$. As this value is higher than the critical value, we reject the null hypothesis (H_0), and we conclude that errors are heterocedastic.

---

[4] Aside from this one, we have also considered other explanatory variables, and the LM test result has always indicated the rejection of homocedasticity hypothesis.

As a consequence, the estimators for the *logistic-regression* coefficients are no longer the most efficient. To obtain consistent estimators for estimators variance, we followed the Huber-White procedure provided by E-Views. The results obtained are shown in table 65; Huber-White procedure corrects only the variance estimators, not modifying the previously presented estimates for the coefficients.

In spite of the correction to the variances, estimates for the coefficients are all statistically significant, confirming the statistical relevance of the explanatory variables considered.

Table 66. E-Views output showing the Huber-White procedure to obtain logistic-regression coefficients

```
Dependent variable: COD
Method: ML - binary Logit (Quadratic hill climbing)
Sample 1: 3200
Included observations: 3200
Convergence achieved after 23 iterations
Covariance matrix computed using second derivatives
```

Variable	Coefficient	Std. error	z-statistic	Prob.
V_CO_SCORING	0.066500	0.003795	17.52427	0.0000
V_CO_CREDIT_LIMIT	0.000621	2.05E-05	12.74539	0.0000
V_CO_CURRENT_BALANCE	0.000499	0.000110	4.52673	0.0000
M_PROFITABILITY	-0.008396	0.002934	2.861424	0.0042
AGE	0.018678	0.007091	2.634029	0.0084
QUALIFIC_D	-0.602927	0.132102	4.564096	0.0000
CI_CO_CLASS_D	-1.43407	0.349123	4.107634	0.0000
V_CO_REVOLVING	-0.000384	0.000120	3.201036	0.0014
MARITAL_STATUS_D	-0.578892	0.134513	4.303619	0.0000
GENDER_D	0.808648	0.14411	5.599634	0.0000
C	-49.8929	2.752544	-18.1261	0.0000
McFadden R-squared	0.653876	Mean dependent var		0.500000
S.D. Dependent var	0.500078	S.E. Of regression		0.260019
Akaike info criterion	0.486704	Sum squared resid		767.7269
Schwartz criterion	0.507573	Log likelihood		2218.071
Hannan-Quinn criter.	0.494186	Restr.log likelihood		0.239915
LR statistic	2.900.688	Avg.log likelihood		
Prob(LR statistic)	0.000000			
Obs with Dep=0	1600	Total obs		3200
Obs with Dep=1	1600			

8.9 Model Validation through Out-of-Sample

The values obtained for the independent variables entered into the model are the following:

Table 67. Coefficient values of the independent variables

Variables in the equation	Code	
v_co_scoring	A	0.066500
v_co_credit_limit	B	0.000261
v_co_current_balance	C	0.000499
m_profitability	D	-0.008396
Age	E	0.018678
Qualific (D)	F	-0.602927
ci_co_class (D)	G	-1.434070
v_co_revolving	H	-0.000384
Marital Status (D)	I	-0.578892
Gender (D)	J	0.808648
Constant		-49.89290

Model validation was made through a sample (*out-of-sample*) with 800 customers (400 good and 400 bad), and it was applied to the *logistic-regression* model according to the following equation:

$$p(Y_i = 1) = \frac{1}{1 + e^{-Z_i}} + \varepsilon_i$$

[43]

$$Z_i = \alpha + \beta_1 x_{1_i} + \ldots + \beta_k x_{k_i}$$

$$Z_i = (- 49.89290 + 0.066500 \times A + 0.000261 \times B + 0.000499 \times C - 0.008396 \times D + 0.018678 \times E - 0.602927 \times \\ - 1.434070 \times G - 0.000384 \times H - 0.578892 \times I - 0{,}808648 \times J)$$

$$p(Y_1 = 1) = \frac{1}{1 + e^{-(- 49.89290 + 0.066500 \times A + 0.000261 \times B + 0.000499 \times C - 0.008396 \times D + 0.018678 \times E - 0.602927 \times F \\ - 1.434070 \times G - 0.000384 \times H - 0.578892 \times I - 0{,}808648 \times J)}}$$

The values obtained are summarized in table 68, which proves the robustness of predictive model.

Table 68. In-sample results

			Predicted		
			COD		
			0	1	Correct %
COD	0		1433	126	89,56%
	1		167	1474	92,13%
		Overall Perc			90,84%
		Total	1600	1600	

Table 69. Out-of-sample results

			Predicted		
			COD		
			0	1	Correct %
COD	0		348	27	87.00%
	1		52	373	93.25%
		Overall Perc			90.13%
		Total	400	400	

8.10 Conclusions

From the similarity of the results obtained in the two samples (*in-sample* and *out-of-sample*), it was demonstrated that the model offers a considerable predictive robustness, anticipating good or bad user outcome, and, thus, anticipating and reducing future doubtful debts.

References

Allison, P. D. 2005. *Logistic Regression Using SAS: Theory and Application*. Cary, North Caroline: SAS Institute Inc.

Altman, E. I. 1968. "Financial Ratios. Discriminant Analysis and the Prediction of Corporate Bankruptcy." *Journal of Finance* 23 (4): 589–609.

Altman, E. I., and A. Saunders. 1998. "Financial Ratios. Discriminant Analysis and the Prediction of Corporate Bankruptcy."*Journal of Banking and Finance* 21: 1721–1742.

Altman, E. I., R. G. Haldeman, and P. Narayanan. 1977. "ZETA Analysis: A New Model to Identify Bankruptcy Risk of Corporations." *Journal of Banking and Finance* 1: 29–54.

Altman, I. E., and E. Hotchkiss. 2006. *Corporate Financial Distress and Bankruptcy*. Third edition. Hoboken, New Jersey: John Wiley & Sons, Inc.

Anderson, R. 2007. *The Credit Scoring Toolkit: Theory and Practice for Retail Credit Risk Management and Decision Automation*. New York: Oxford University Press.

Aziz, A., and G. H. Lawson. 1989. "Cash flow reporting and financial distress models." *Ph.D Dissertation.*

Batista, A. Sarmento. 2004. *A Gestão do Crédito como Vantagem Competitiva*. Third edition. Porto: Vida Económica.

Batista, A. Sarmento. 2012. *Credit Scoring*. Porto: Vida Económica

Beaver, W. 1966. "Financial Ratios as Predictors of Bankruptcy." *Journal of Accounting Research* 6: 71–102.

Crook, J. N., R. Hamilton, and L. C Thomas. 1992. "A comparison of a credit scoring model with a credit performance model." *The Service Industries Journal* 558-579.

Demaris, A. 1990. "Interpreting logistic regression results: A critical commentary." *Journal of Marriage and the Family* 52: 271–277.

Dimitras, A. I., S. H. Zanakis, and C. Zopounidis. 1996. "A survey of business failures with an emphasis on prediction methods and industrial applications." *European Journal of Operational Research* 90: 487–513.

Eisenbeis, R. A. 1978. "Problems in applyng discriminant analysis in credit scoring models." *Journal of Banking Finance* 2: 205–219.

Espahbodi, H., and P. Espahbodi. 2003. "Binary choice models and corporate takeover." *Journal of Banking and Finance* 27: 549–574.

Fair Isaac. 2006. *A discussion of Data Analysis: Prediction and Decision Techniques.* San Rafael: FICO Edit.

Freed, N., and F. Glover. 1981. "A linear programming approach to the discriminant problem." *Decision Sci.* 12: 68–74.

Freed, N., and F. Glover. 1981. "Simple but powerful goal programming formulation for the discriminant problem." *European J. Oper. Res.* 7: 44–60.

Frydman, H., E. I. Altman, and D. Kao. 1985. "Introducing Recursive Partitioning for Financial Classification: The Case of Financial Distress." *Journal of Finance* 11: 269–291.

Greene, W.H. 2002. *Econometric analysis.* Upper Saddle River, New Jersey: Prentice Hall

Gross, D. B., and N. S. Souleles. 2002. "An Empirical Analysis of Personal Bankruptcy and Delinquency." *Review of Financial Studies* 15: 319–347.

Hand, D. J. 2001. "Modelling consumer credit risk." *IMA Journal of Management Mathematics* 12, 173-200.

Hand, D. J., and W. E. Henley. 1997. "Statistical classification methods in consumer credit scoring: a review." *J.R. Statist. Soc. A* 160, part 3: 523–541.

Hanley, J. A., and B. J. McNeil. 1983. "A method of comparing the areas under receiver operating characteristics curves derived from the same cases." *Radiology* 148 (3): 839–843.

Hayden, E. 2002. "Modeling an Accounting-Based Rating System for Austrian Firms." 125 f. Dissertation (Doktor der Sozial und Wirtschaftswissenschaften). University of Vienna, Vienna, Austria.

Henley, W. E. 1995. "Statistical Aspects of Credit Scoring." Ph.D. Thesis, Open University, Milton Keynes, U.K.

Kleinbaum, G. David, and Klein Mitchel. 2010. *Logistic Regression—A self-Learning Text*. Third edition. Springer.

Lewis, E. M. 1992. *An Introduction to Credit Scoring*. San Rafael, California: Fair Isaac and Co. Inc.

Menard, S. 1995. "Applied Logistic Regression Analysis." *Sage University Papers Series on Quantitative Application in the Social Sciences,* series 07-106.

Müller, M., H. Kraft, and G. Kroisandt. 2002. "Assessing Discriminatory Power of Credit Rating." *Discussion Paper No 67, Sonderforschungsbereich 373,* Humbolt-University Berlin.

Ohlson, J. A. 1980. "Financial Ratios and the Probabilistic Prediction of Bankruptcy." *Journal of Economic Theory* 79: 1–45; *e Journal of Accounting Research*, 18: 109–131.

Ooghe, H., and S. Balcaen. 2002. "Are failure prediction models transferable from one country to another? An empirical study using Belgian financial statements." *Vlerick Working Papers* 2002/5.

Pampel, C. Fred. 2000. "Logistic Regression, a Primer." A SAGE University Paper 132.

Persons, O. S. 1999. "Using financial information to differentiate failed *vs.* surviving finance companies in Thailand: an implication for emerging economies." *Multinational Finance Journal* 3 (2): 127–145.

Platt, H. D., and M. B. Platt. 2002. "Predicting corporate financial distress: reflections on choice-based sample bias." *Journal of Economics and Finance* 26, 184-199.

Press, S. J., and S. Wilson. 1978. "Choosing Between Logistic Regression and Discriminant Analysis." *Journal of the American Statistical Association, JSTOR.vol.73. No364, pp 699-705.*

Reis, E. 2001. *Estatística Multivariada Aplicada.* Second edition. Lisboa: Edições Sílabo.

Schewe, G., and J. Leker. J. Hauschildt and Leker, eds. 2000. *Statistische Insolvenzdiagnose: Diskriminanzanalyse versus logistische Regression.* Second edition. Köln: Krisendiagnose durch Bilanzanalyse.

Siddiqi, N. 2006. *Credit Risk Scorecards: Developing and Implementing Intelligent Credit Scoring.* Hoboken, New Jersey: John Wiley & Sons, Inc.

Thomas, L. C. 2009. *Consumer Credit Models. Pricing, Profit and Portfolios.* Oxford: Oxford University Press.

Thomas, L. C., D. B. Edelman, and J. N. Crook. 2002. *Credit Scoring and Its Applications.* Philadelphia: SIAM Monographs on Mathematical Modeling and Computation.

Thomas, L. C., D. B. Edelman, and J. N. Crook. 2006. *Readings in Credit Scoring: Recent developments, advances and aims.* Oxford: Oxford University Press.

Wiginton, J. C. 1980. "A note on the comparison of *logit* and discriminant models of consumer credit behavior." *Journal of Financial Quantitative Analysis* 15: 757–770.

Wilson, N., B. Summers, and R. Hope. 2000. "Using payment behavior data for credit risk modeling." *International Journal of the Economics of Business* 7 (3): 333–346.

Zavgren, C. V., and E. Friedman. 1988. "Are bankruptcy prediction models worthwhile? An application in securities analysis." *Management International Review* 18, pp55-63.

www.ingramcontent.com/pod-product-compliance
Lightning Source LLC
Chambersburg PA
CBHW051705170526
45167CB00002B/542